Creating Multi-sensory Enviro

'This book will offer a whole new world of sensory experience for all students. The author, Christopher Davies, fully appreciates the time demands on school staff. His instructions are meticulous and detailed – offering total solutions for busy teachers to create stimulating learning environments. Be prepared to be "wowed".'
Lorraine Petersen, CEO of nasen

'As an experienced teacher still working in the classroom after twenty years I know I will use this book.'
John Naylor, Advanced Skills Teacher, Yeoman Park School

'This book provides a treasure chest of ways to motivate and engage children and the adults working with them. It is accessible to anyone and with a minimum of resources can be used to create memorable learning environments and magical moments. Be prepared to be inspired and re-energised!'
Isobel Dearman, Deputy Headteacher, Hillcrest School

This highly practical guide to creating and using multi-sensory environments is packed full of ideas for low-cost, easy to assemble multi-sensory environments, accompanied with suggestions for use with clear learning outcomes linked to the P levels for children with special educational needs.

These creative learning environments, focussing on multi-sensory experiences:

- include suggestions for extension or differentiation depending on the abilities of your students, or the time available;
- are designed to stimulate all the sensory channels – auditory, visual, kinaesthetic, olfactory and gustatory;
- encourage creative thinking and learning, and development of social and emotional skills;
- can be set up in your classroom or school hall, some of them in just a matter of minutes;
- can be a semi-permanent feature in a small area of the classroom, convenient for use at any given moment;
- provide theory and background to multi-sensory learning to enable you to adapt the suggested scenarios according to the needs of individual learners.

Although these activities will be of particular value for children with sensory impairments, they will also provide stimulating learning environments, as promoted in the themes and principles of the Early Years Foundation Stage guidance.

Christopher Davies is Artistic Director of Bamboozle, which works with children who have a range of SEN. The company runs theatre arts residencies, delivers trainings and produces interactive multi-sensory touring shows for special schools. Bamboozle works in partnership with schools to develop creative ways of engaging students who are at the hard to reach end of the autistic spectru ... ways staff approach the curriculum.

nasen (National Association for Special Educational Needs) is a professional membership association that supports all those who work with or care for children and young people with special and additional educational needs. Members include teachers, teaching assistants, support workers, other educationalists, students and parents.

nasen supports its members through policy documents, journals, its magazine Special!, publications, professional development courses, regional networks and newsletters. Its website contains more current information such as responses to government consultations. **nasen**'s published documents are held in very high regard both in the UK and internationally.

Other titles published in association with nasen:

Forthcoming titles:

Language for Learning in the Secondary School: A Practical Guide for Supporting Students with Speech, Language and Communication Needs
Sue Hayden and Emma Jordan
2012/pb: 978–0–415–61975–2

ADHD: All Your Questions Answered: A Complete Handbook for SENCOs and Teachers
Fintan O'Regan
2012/pb: 978–0–415–59770–8

Assessing Children with Specific Learning Difficulties: A Teacher's Practical Guide
Gavin Reid, Gad Elbeheri and John Everatt
2012/pb: 978–0–415–67027–2

Using Playful Practice to Communicate with Special Children
Margaret Corke
2012/pb: 978–0–415–68767–6

The Equality Act for Educational Professionals: A Simple Guide to Disability and Inclusion in Schools
Geraldine Hills
2012/pb: 978–0–415–68768–3

More Trouble with Maths: A Teacher's Complete Guide to Identifying and Diagnosing Mathematical Difficulties
Steve Chinn
2012/pb: 978–0–415–67013–5

Dyslexia and Inclusion: Classroom Approaches for Assessment, Teaching and Learning
Gavin Reid
2012/pb: 978–0–415–60758–2

Available now:
Brilliant Ideas for Using ICT in the Inclusive Classroom
Sally McKeown and Angela McGlashon
2011/pb: 978–0–415–67254–2

The SENCO Survival Guide: The Nuts and Bolts of Everything You Need to Know
Sylvia Edwards
2010/pb: 978–0–415–59281–9

The SEN Handbook for Trainee Teachers, NQTs and Teaching Assistants
Wendy Spooner
2010/pb: 978–0–415–56771–8

Attention Deficit Hyperactivity Disorder: What Can Teachers Do?
Geoff Kewley
2010/pb: 978–0–415–49202–7

Young People with Anti-Social Behaviours: Practical Resources for Professionals
Kathy Hampson
2010/pb: 978–0–415–56570–7

Confronting Obstacles to Inclusion: International Responses to Developing Inclusive Education
Richard Rose
2010/pb: 978–0–415–49363–5

Supporting Children's Reading: A Complete Short Course for Teaching Assistants, Volunteer Helpers and Parents
Margaret Hughes and Peter Guppy
2010/pb: 978–0–415–49836–4

Dyspraxia 5–14: Identifying and Supporting Young People with Movement Difficulties
Christine Macintyre
2009/pb: 978–0–415–54396–5

A Handbook for Inclusion Managers: Steering Your School Towards Inclusion
Ann Sydney
2009/pb: 978–0–415–49198–3

Living With Dyslexia: The Social and Emotional Consequences of Specific Learning Difficulties/Disabilities
Barbara Riddick and Angela Fawcett
2009/pb: 978–0–415–47758–1

'This book provides an excellent treasure chest of ways to create environments that motivate and engage children, young people and the adults working with them. It is accessible to anyone and often with the minimum of resources. Christopher uses a tried and tested formula that can be adapted to meet the needs of individuals to create memorable learning and possible magical moments. The non-judgemental approaches advocated in the book gives children and young people the confidence to surprise us with what they are capable of achieving. This is a book all about having a go. Be prepared to be inspired and re-energised!'

Isobel Dearman, Deputy Headteacher, Hillcrest School

'As a Newly Qualified Teacher I would have been very happy to have come across this book. The thing that impresses me most . . . is its promotion of the idea that teachers as well as students can be learners in creative partnership.'

John Naylor, Advanced Skills Teacher, Yeoman Park School, Nottinghamshire

Creating Multi-sensory Environments

Practical ideas for
teaching and learning

Christopher Davies

Routledge
Taylor & Francis Group

LONDON AND NEW YORK

Helping Everyone Achieve

First published 2012
by Routledge
2 Park Square, Milton Park, Abingdon, Oxon OX14 4RN

Simultaneously published in the USA and Canada
by Routledge
711 Third Avenue, New York, NY 10017

Routledge is an imprint of the Taylor & Francis Group, an informa business

British Library Cataloguing in Publication Data
A catalogue record for this book is available from the British Library

Library of Congress Cataloging in Publication Data
Davies, Christopher.
  Creating multisensory environments : practical ideas for teaching and learning / by Christopher Davies.
      p. cm.
  Includes bibliographical references and index.
  1. Perceptual-motor learning—Audio-visual aids. 2. Sensory stimulation—Great Britain. 3. Children with disabilities—Education—Great Britain. 4. Classroom environment—Great Britain. I. Title.
  LB1067.D38 2012
  371.102′4—dc23   2011028731

ISBN: 978–0–415–57329–0 (hbk)
ISBN: 978–0–415–57330–6 (pbk)
ISBN: 978–0–203–14188–5 (ebk)

Typeset in Bembo
by Swales & Willis Ltd, Exeter, Devon

Printed and bound in Great Britain by
TJ International Ltd, Padstow, Cornwall

For:
Lily and Hayley
Amy and Iona
remarkable people
and
valued friends of Bamboozle
Thank you

Contents

Foreword

Multi-sensory environments have been used very successfully in our special schools for many years. Often the perception is that you have to have a room with very expensive equipment to offer light, sound and sensory stimulation. The cost of such equipment and the inability to find a dedicated room to use within a school has meant that many schools have decided this is not for them.

This book will make all those schools think again. It offers practical solutions to creating multi-sensory environments within classrooms, corridors and hallways at a fraction of the cost of installing expensive equipment.

The book begins with ideas and suggestions for creating spaces using structures and fixtures, ideas for defining space and dividing areas as well as making entrances more engaging.

The author, Christopher Davies, fully appreciates the time demands on school staff and has tried to offer support and guidance that will enable teachers to create stimulating, multi-sensory environments. Whilst working with teachers he has learnt that the three key barriers to establishing multi-sensory environments are time, cost and usefulness. Within the pages of this book Christopher offers really practical examples of how to remove those barriers in order to create useful environments quickly and cheaply.

His instructions are meticulous and detailed offering total solutions for busy teachers to create stimulating learning environments.

The flexibility of the instructions means that each teacher can make adaptations to meet the needs of individual students. Guidance is also provided on whether the environment will need to be put together by an adult or where possible for students to be involved in their construction.

For some students, there can be an over-stimulation of one of the senses and this is addressed by making it very clear that every teacher needs to know and understand the requirements of each individual student and ensure they are best placed to determine the most effective way of introducing stimuli.

The instructions will support teachers in making those professional judgements as well as supporting the reader in making health and safety decisions in regard to students' needs and the accessibility of the multi-sensory environment.

Although there are over twenty different environments described in this book the instructions for their development all follow the same pattern. These include the different sensory aspects that will be stimulated, the equipment needed, how to put it together, how to use it and the learning outcomes that could be achieved. This will support teachers with their planning and will offer guidance for support staff working alongside individual students.

The inspiration for this book has come from thousands of students, school staff and families that the author has worked with over a number of years. Within the pages of this book he shares those ideas to enable many more students to benefit from the stimulating, exciting and inspiring learning environments that he has described.

Christopher talks about creating the 'wow' factor as students first enter a room in order to inspire and excite the learning experience. This book, whilst offering practical solutions, will also offer a whole new world of sensory experience for all students.

Be prepared to be 'wowed'.

Lorraine Petersen, CEO of nasen

Acknowledgements

This book is the result of ideas I have collected and developed while teaching in the classroom, when working as part of the Leicestershire drama advisory team and, most significantly, since setting up Bamboozle in 1994. During that time I have been privileged to work with many, many inspirational people who have all contributed in some way to the book by their willing exploration of, and engagement with, the collection of multisensory ideas that are distilled here. These include a huge number of families who have a child with learning difficulties, many staff in special schools across the country, the Bamboozle board of trustees and admin team and so many artists who have brought their creativity to the work. And, maybe most significantly, thousands of young people who have learning difficulties with whom we have worked and played. A huge and heartfelt thank you to all of you.

Specifically thanks too are due to:
Corallie Murray, David Lloyd (Bamboozle trustees) and Susan Pešić Smith for early advice; Chris White for writing the learning outcomes sections and attributing P levels to the activities; staff at Birkett House School for advice on the layout of the activity pages; Hayley Smith and Iona Mayo (Bamboozle trustees) and their daughters Lily and Amy from whom I have learnt so much; Alison Foyle at Routledge/David Fulton for editorial guidance and encouragement; Caroline Watson from Swales & Willis for advice on layout; and to Lorraine Petersen, CEO of nasen, for writing the Foreword. Photographs are by Jonny Thatcher, Gemma Mount and Peter Whelan.

Finally, and most significantly, to Sue Pyecroft, co-artistic director of Bamboozle, the illustrator and my wife for her treasured support, ideas and patience.

So you can see that I have had a lot of direct and indirect help with this book for which I am truly grateful. Any omissions or inaccuracies however remain entirely down to me.

Introduction

The inspiration for this book has come from the thousands of students, school staff and families I have met and worked with since 1994 when I became co-artistic director of Bamboozle Theatre Company. We have often been asked to put down our ideas so that more students, staff and parents can have access to them. And now I have!

The ideas that I describe are practical; they have all been used with students who have varying degrees of learning abilities and disabilities. Some are simple, some have more elements to them (see Figures 1 and 2 below). They all have been developed during Bamboozle residencies and touring productions and owe a great deal to the creativity and dedication of our artists, the advice of teachers, support staff and parents and, crucially, to the students who have contributed to the contents of this book in ways they don't realise. It is after all the responses of the students that really determine whether an idea works or not.

The environments and activities are designed to inspire and intrigue students, staff and parents alike – to create the 'wow' factor when first entering the room. If we can bring our students into an exciting and different setting then any work that goes on will be enhanced.

Planning and creating such stimulating multi-sensory spaces for activities to take place in can be a time-consuming activity. Time is something that is often in short supply for teachers and support staff in special schools. What this book aims to do is to provide some ideas and short cuts so that you can create simple and stimulating environments within your classroom or school hall. As you read through the environments and activities you will see that some of them can be set up and cleared away in a few minutes while others take longer.

The environments can be used at many different levels. For example each setting is designed to have visual, auditory and kinaesthetic stimuli and to be an intriguing space to enter. Some of the environments have the capacity to raise questions, are able to pose problems, and can become a setting for activity, such as for a character to inhabit, or simply for the participants to interact with.

Each environment has been carefully put together to be multi-sensory – to be accessible to participants who may not be able to see very well, those who can't hear or those who have tactile aversions. We provide lots of different stimuli within each environment (live and recorded music and sound, interesting objects, a variety of materials and textures, a range of lighting effects, olfactory stimuli etc.) to ensure that every individual participant can engage with, or be challenged by, at least some of the elements within it.

Figure 1 A simple activity can give a rich experience. Here clay mixed with water provides a soothing cool experience for both the giver and receiver of the massage.

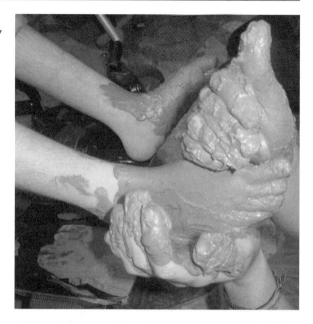

Figure 2 A more complex setting gives many multi-sensory opportunities. This collection of simple materials with a few authentic artefacts added makes an interesting **visual** display that could be part of a farmyard environment as in Chapter 22, Circle of Straw Bales. It also has **auditory** potential with the sound of buckets and the milk churn; **kinaesthetic** experiences, handling the hay; **olfactory** with the smell of hay, carrots and celery; and **gustatory** ones if the vegetables are eaten as well as offered to a horse!

The environments are also designed to be flexible. For some students, particularly some of those on the autistic spectrum, one stimulus at a time is often, but by no means always, more appropriate. You will see in the section 'How to use this book' below how each chapter is designed to enable you to quickly find the particular sense you wish to focus on or the part of the environment that suits the particular needs of your students.

I do hope you enjoy using the ideas as much as I have enjoyed putting them together for you. Have fun!

Christopher Davies
May 2011

Christopher Davies is co-artistic director of Bamboozle Theatre Company which works across the UK and beyond with students who have learning disabilities and those with emotional and behavioural difficulties. The company runs residencies for special schools and for families who have a child with profound and complex needs or one who is on the autistic spectrum. It tours productions for small audiences to special schools, runs a wide-reaching training programme for school staff and theatre practitioners and works with schools to effect culture change. Bamboozle also produces resources including books, teacher packs, CDs, DVDs and other materials. Co-artistic director Christopher Davies publishes free fortnightly emailed newsletters with multi-sensory activities, drama ideas and behaviour management strategies.

www.bamboozletheatre.co.uk

How to use this book

I suggest reading Section one – Getting started before going on to any of the specific environments and activities in Section two. This is because what is described in Section one will help in the setting up of the environments for the activities.

I am conscious that the demands on school staff mean that time for setting up environments like some of those described in this book can be in short supply. I have therefore in many cases explained things in more detail than you might need. This is an attempt to be clear and to make it easy – to reduce any guesswork you need to employ. It goes without saying that you may well want to just collect the materials and put them up in your own way to suit your own needs.

I'd like you to always keep in mind that the settings themselves and the suggestions for using them are just that; suggestions. One of the many teachers who helped me with the contents said: *'It is not the environment so much as how we work in it with our own students. Every teacher will use their own professional judgement as well as the knowledge of their own students to modify the ideas.'*

Each of the activities from 1–23 stands alone and they can therefore be dipped into in any order you like. They are laid out with these headings:

Title: e.g. 1. Musical Forest

Immediately beneath the title is my view about whether the environment is best suited to be set up by staff or whether you can involve the students in its construction. Involving students in creating the environment for an activity has the potential to draw them into the drama as they are part of creating the setting in which it is going to happen. This has to be balanced with the impact that coming into a magical multi-sensory garden or a war zone can have. It is a judgement call for you; you will know your students and your intentions, so are best placed to decide. Both have their merits.

Then there are seven sections for each activity as follows.

1. **What is set up as your students enter the room**
   This is designed to give you an immediate overview of the environment and a brief guide to some of its potential uses.
2. **Different sensory channels**
   This section divides up the contents of each chapter into four parts. The three principal senses – visual, auditory and kinaesthetic – have a part each, while the olfactory and gustatory senses are put together. This means that you are able to see at a glance how rich the environment is for any particular sense. For example if you have a number of V.I. students then clearly the auditory and kinaesthetic opportunities are going to be more appropriate than the visual.
3. **Equipment needed**
   This section lists what you will need to set up the environment and engage in the activities. It groups them under the different sensory headings as (2) (above). Many items of equipment fall into more than one category. For example a shell has visual and kinaesthetic qualities and sometimes auditory too – in these cases I have included them in the section that seems to me to be the most appropriate.
   You can of course make use of as many or as few of the suggestions as serves your purpose.
4. **How to put it together**
   This section gives a step-by-step method to put together the suggested environment.
5. **Ways to make use of it**
   Here I have suggested just some of the many ways it is possible to use each environment. The list is by no means exhaustive and I imagine that you will have additional ideas.
6. **The environments in action**
   In this section I describe one example of how each environment has been used.
7. **Suggested learning outcomes: P Scales**
   The use of Performance Scales is now well established for pupils working below Level 1 of the National Curriculum. The descriptors for P1–P3 are generic statements that can be applied to performance across a range of subjects. Descriptors for P4–P8, however, follow more subject specific lines. Although there are no specific descriptors for drama-based activities, given the purpose of this book, we have decided to mainly use elements from the Speaking and Listening strands. Where other strands are apparent, such as in the construction of props or in follow-up activities, we have also signposted descriptors to Maths, Art, Science etc.

Importantly, the levels we suggest are just that, suggestions. As the P Scales are progressive, professionals working day-in-day-out with pupils can very easily attribute any activity to any P Scale at any level. This is especially true with Speaking and Listening targets, for example an activity where a student meets and engages with a character could work at P4 'Pupils respond to requests at one key word' or P5 'to follow requests with two key words' and even P6 'requests at three key words'. The judgement that the professional would give is dependent on the pupil's abilities and responses.

Level descriptors have been taken from 'Performance – P Level attainment targets', published by QCA, July 2007.

P levels are shown at the bottom of each activity where they can be measured and then repeated as a list at the bottom of each environment for ease of reference.

Multi-sensory stimuli

We have left you to make the judgement about how many of the multi-sensory stimuli are used simultaneously. For some students, for example those on the autistic spectrum, beginning with a blank canvas and introducing sensory activities one at a time might be most suitable. Others, such as those on the MLD spectrum, may thoroughly enjoy and be engaged by a richer and more varied sensory experience for a short time. My view is that you will be the best judge of which approach is suitable for which of your students.

Wheelchair users

In the interests of simplicity I have not generally indicated which activities are suitable for wheelchair users and which require the participants to be ambulant. This is because I anticipate that you, the reader, will again be the best judge of that. For example, I might have assumed that crawling through a tunnel under a classroom table is not suitable for wheelchair users, which would not allow for the likelihood that some wheelchair users can pull themselves along the floor on their arms and would love and benefit from the chance to do so through a tunnel underneath a table. So I leave it to you to make such judgements.

In some places, however, I do suggest some minor adjustments to a setting that would enable it to be made available to those using wheelchairs.

Smoke machines

Using a smoke machine can enhance the experience in many of the environments and activities. Some students for example will watch drifting smoke vapours in the air for very long periods of time (Figure 3). Smoke also adds significant atmosphere to certain

Figure 3
A smoke machine gives added atmosphere to many environments. Students often watch lingering wisps of smoke for some time.

environments including: Chapter 4, Rainforest Jungle; Chapter 7, Snowfield; Chapter 12, Trenches of World War I; Chapter 13, Snow Queen's Castle; and Chapter 23, Border Crossing.

Caution: smoke machines vary. The one we use creates the smoke effect by using a vegetable oil vapour that has no allergenic side effects. There can be a problem in some schools with setting off the fire alarm. You will need to check this before using a smoke machine. Fire alarm systems do vary and some are set off by our machine but many are not. In some cases the alarm in the school hall for instance can be isolated for the duration of the session when the smoke machine is in use. Beware of smoke escaping from the room that has been isolated to another part of the building where the alarm is still activated.

Creating a non-judgemental space for learning

A non-judgemental space is one in which students can interact with environments, with each other and with us, the facilitators and teachers, without the slightest fear of being judged – of getting it wrong.

If we can create such a space it is my belief that students, whatever their abilities and disabilities, will flourish in ways that we might not have thought possible.

We are all in the business of encouraging students. The question is how to do it. How can we encourage and still enhance the fear-free environment that characterises a non-judgemental space. If we encourage students by saying 'good' or 'well done' what we are actually doing is giving credit to them for meeting our agenda. 'Good – you have guessed what I think is the right answer so I am giving you credit. Well done.' What this does is to give the message that there is a right answer out there and I, the adult around here, know what it is and it is your job to guess what it is. This encourages a guessing game which is by its nature judgemental – you guess right or you guess wrong. Some students when faced with this tend to stop offering suggestions in case they fail. So the question remains: how can we encourage without being judgemental?

If we can frame questions and invitations in such a way that there is a spirit of joint enquiry we give the message that we are in this together and an opinion offered is going to be given attention and valued. The trick is to avoid questions that have a right answer.

Some of the activities described in this book use questions and statements and make invitations (with words or without) that do not have a right answer. For example:

- **'I wonder what was going on there?'** The great thing about 'wonder' is that we can wonder anything at all: I wonder if the moon is made of cheese? It makes no sense to ask if a wondering is right or wrong – I was only wondering.
- **'What do we think she might be feeling?'** We can think what we like without considering whether it is so or not – and she might be feeling anything.
- **'What did anyone notice?'** Different people will notice different things; we are all entitled to notice what we notice without being judged.
- **'The invitation is for any of you to go up and have a look at the castle'.** The lovely thing about invitations is that they can be accepted or declined. Anyone can accept the invitation to look at the castle or stay where they are.

Asking such questions and making such invitations in this way contributes to a sense of joint exploration and creates an encouraging environment in which to work. There is always the possibility that a student declines an invitation. This has to be accepted by us otherwise the students are simply doing what we tell them and do not have the opportunity to set their own agenda. Just because I have spent time creating a wonderful multisensory experience does not mean that any individual has to take advantage of it. It is my experience that the less I try to 'encourage' someone to handle an object, meet a character or get involved in some action the more they want to do it.

The less I judge what students do the more they seem to want to get involved.

Use of terminology and acronyms

Terminology

Students
In the interests of simplicity I have used the term 'students' throughout to denote the children and young people for whom these environments are created and activities devised.

Him or her
When giving examples of a student doing something I have alternated my use of her and him rather than put 'him or her' on each occasion. I have not been fastidious about how many times I have used either – I trust it will be roughly equal!

Learning difficulties or learning disabilities
I have used these terms more or less interchangeably.

Residency
By residency I mean a period of time (often a week in Bamboozle's case) when an artist or theatre company are 'in residence' at a theatre or school to work with a group of students on a certain theme.

Props
Short for properties and a term used in theatre for any object that is used during the action or activity.

Newsprint
The paper used to print newspapers and acquired as end of rolls from newspaper printing houses for free.

Acronyms

I have used the following acronyms and abbreviations:

PMLD   Profound and multiple learning difficulties
SLD   Severe learning difficulties

MLD	Moderate learning difficulties
EBD	Emotional and behavioural difficulties
ASD	Autistic spectrum disorders
V.I.	Visual impaired
TA	Teaching assistant – in school
P Scales	Performance Scales
P Levels	Performance Levels

Section one

Getting started

This section is about what we can do before we actually begin putting up a multi-sensory environment or starting an activity. In it I will explain how to:

- **use structures for creating spaces:** how you can put up permanent fixtures in the classroom to make creating the environments quick and easy;
- **define the space:** ways to create a neutral space by dividing part of the room — so that the part of the room you are going to work in is clearly defined;
- **make entrances engaging:** how to make the entrance to the room intriguing.

Structures for creating spaces

In a theatre there is a series of bars crossing the roof above the stage from which lights and scenery are suspended. Such a purpose-built facility is not available in classrooms but we can create something that will give similar possibilities. This section has ideas that will enable you to easily hang things from walls, ceiling or doorway and gain height to give a focus to work.

Structures 1

Fixed points around the classroom

This idea is designed to simplify the transformation of a room into a rich and exciting multi-sensory environment.

What is needed is a number of fixed points around the classroom onto which it is possible to attach string or rope. Some classrooms already have brackets on the wall for various reasons that might be able to be utilised – but for many there is nothing that you can attach to. The ideal is to have suspension points all over the ceiling so that you can hang something from anywhere you want to. In practice this is rarely possible; for example many classrooms have suspended ceilings from which it is not advisable to hang things! Others have tracking for hoists that need to be kept free from hangings. One solution is to fix a number of heavy-duty cup hooks or eyelets into the walls at near ceiling height. The more you have the more options you create. A hook in each corner and one in the centre of each wall gives lots of opportunities to tie lengths of thin rope across the ceiling at various angles. The rope can then have material, a camouflage net or anything reasonably light that you choose suspended from it. The size and security of fixing will determine the weight you are able to hang onto the rope without it sagging too much.

Pulley system

One way around the sagging problem is to have a cleat on the wall below some of the fixings. This enables you to run the rope from the hook at one side of the room through the eyelet on the opposite wall and down to the cleat below it to tie off. You can then pull the string tighter if it stretches when you hang things from it. It also enables you to lower the rope to tie things onto it without having to climb ladders; and you can lower, for example, a camouflage net to the level you need it for a particular activity.

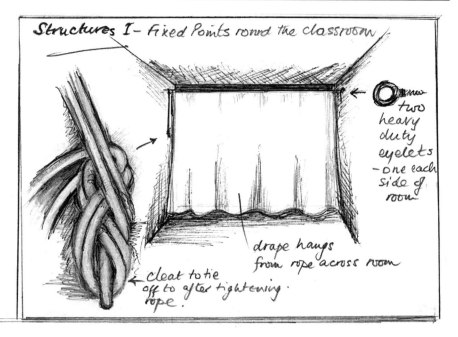

Figure 4 Permanent fixed points round the classroom provide convenient tying off points. This enables many of the environments to be put up quickly.

Structures 2

Hooks at the entrance

Whatever we have at the classroom door (or the entrance to hall or studio) will give a message to the students about what is to come. Hanging something up over the door or putting a notice on it is an excellent way of indicating that something different is going to happen. Fixing two cup hooks above the door, one on each side, enables you to easily put something up and take it down. A garden cane with material attached works well as it can be quickly put up by resting it on the hooks and equally quickly taken down. This can be used as a visual clue that this lesson is drama, or storytelling, or art and craft etc.

See Entrances 1 – Doorways (page 18) for examples of using this structure

Structures 3

Creating height

I find it useful to have a way of creating height in a classroom or studio for drama activities, storytelling or indeed for displaying creative work.

One simple way is to have a base with a pole inserted into it. This is easily stored, simple to erect and provides a flexible vehicle for a number of activities. For example:

- You can attach branches to it spreading from the central pole to create a tree that can be used for a character to sit under, to display artwork such as model birds.

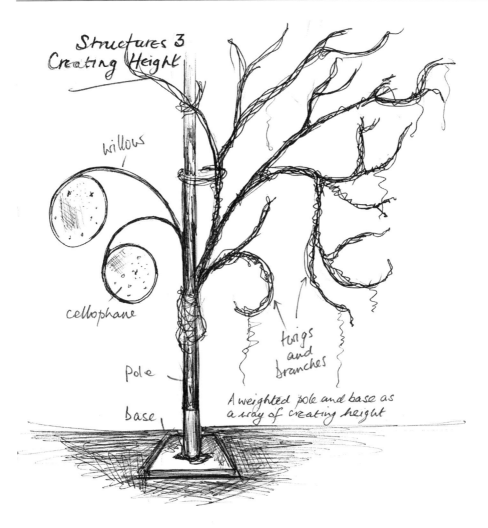

Structures 3
Creating Height

willows

cellophane

Pole

base

twigs
and
branches

A weighted pole and base as
a way of creating height

Figure 5 Having a way of creating height in the classroom is a very useful facility for many of the activities in Section two. Here a pole and base is used as the basis for a tree.

- By attaching a cross pole near the top you can hang a white sheet to represent the sail of a ship.
- Sliding cardboard boxes onto it decorated with Native American images can create a totem pole.

With two or more poles and bases the opportunities for creating settings are multiplied. String or thin rope can be hung between two of them that can be used to hang things from, including:

- lines of washing for a story about a laundry woman – Mrs Jewell in *The King of Capri* for example;

- a simple backdrop for a character to sit in front of, created by suspending a sheet of fabric from the rope. This gives a neutral background to the activity and can help students to focus and concentrate on the activity without the distraction of displays on the wall or someone passing the window.

Depending upon the weight of what you hang from, or attach to, the pole you may need to put additional weight on the bases to ensure they are stable. This could be done by using purpose-made stage weights or improvised with a bag of sand or something similar.

Defining the space

Classrooms are interesting places. Often the walls have displays of work and other visually stimulating materials on them. This can be a distraction for some activities. Keeping students' attention can be daunting when there is so much to look at in addition to what you are inviting them to concentrate on. For some activities, such as drama and storytelling, a much more neutral space is required. Here are three ways to 'clean' the space, clear the clutter from lines of sight and eliminate the possible distractions that are on the walls and a fourth simple way to identify the working space within a classroom.

Defining the space 1

Circle of corrugated card

This is a way of creating an intimate space within a classroom or hall that is ideal for activities that demand concentration and focussed attention from the participants.

By using a roll of corrugated card about 2 metres high (see Figure 6) you can eliminate all the distractions in the room at a stroke and make a clean and clear space in which to tell a story, meet a puppet or pass round a precious object.

This is a very flexible solution as you can roll out enough of the corrugated card to make the space large enough to accommodate your whole group or small enough for an activity with just one or two students. This provides an intimate place without distractions. It also has the potential to create intrigue – 'When is it my turn to go in?' – and a sense of the unknown, especially if the entrance winds a bit so that students can't see in until they have fully entered – 'What's around the corner?' or 'Who am I going to meet in the middle?'

By standing the card in a wavy line you won't need to prop it up – it will be self-supporting. If you have students who are likely to knock into it (accidentally or intentionally) then some way of holding it in position will be needed as – like the proverbial dominoes – once one part is knocked over the rest will follow! You can tape it to the floor every few metres, prop it up against furniture or attach cord to the top of the card and tie it off to the ceiling or walls.

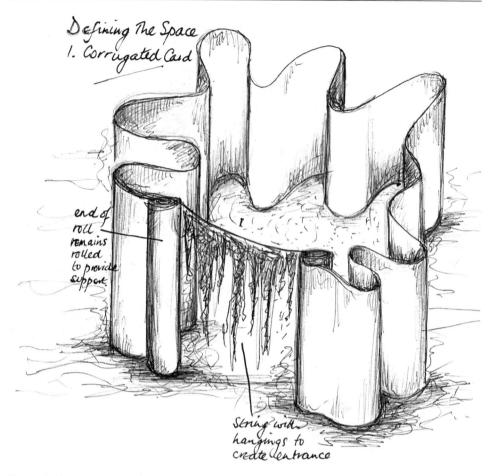

Defining The Space
1. Corrugated Card

end of
roll
remains
rolled
to provide
support

String with
hangings to
create entrance

Figure 6 Here corrugated card is used to define a space. It is a quick way of creating an intimate space for drama or storytelling. When the card is set up in this wavy fashion it is self-supporting.

Defining the space 2

Circle of poles

The second way is to use free-standing poles (see Structures 3 – Creating height, page 12) with ropes suspended between them. You can then hang fabric from the ropes to create a discrete space in which to work. How dense the hangings are will affect the atmosphere created. If you want people from the outside to see something of what is going on inside then hanging thin strips of fabric from the ropes will allow that. If however you require the space inside to be completely secret then hanging sheets of fabric will give this secrecy.

Defining the space 3

Cover the furniture and walls

Another simple and quick way of transforming the look of the classroom is to cover the tables and other furniture with large sheets of newsprint★ or fabric. This can represent a range of mountains, a polar or lunar landscape, or can simply be a blank canvas to use as a backdrop for a story. What it does is quickly change the classroom from the everyday to something extraordinary.

The idea can also be extended to cover the walls too. Simply tape the paper to the walls near the ceiling, allowing the paper to hang down and cover any displays or shelf units against the wall.

It is not just furniture and walls that can be covered in this way. If you have something that you want to reveal later in the session you can have it in place but hidden from view under the newsprint. Large sheets of fabric will do a similar job (see Chapter 19, Bomb Site, page 130).

The newsprint comes on rolls – some about 2m and others 1m long and there is often a lot of paper left on them. One of the great advantages is that it can be used to create an environment very quickly such as creating a neutral space such as described above, and those described in Chapters 7–11 (pages 67–88). You can use it to completely transform the look of the room in a few minutes, create a giant piece of artwork or even screw it up for a snowball fight!

Defining the space 4

Circle of carpet squares

One of the simplest methods of defining a space, and certainly one of the easiest to set up, is to place a circle of carpet squares on the floor. This gives a clear indication to the students where we want them to sit and the action can go on within the circle. Equally, if we have something planned that requires a different shaped space then we can lay the squares out in a semi-circle or a cluster or whatever arrangement is best suited to the activity to come.

A simple space like this can also be made with a circle of chairs or beanbags and cushions.

★ A note on newsprint
Newsprint is, as you can imagine, the paper on which newspapers are printed. It is a great material for all sorts of uses – and it is free. Your local newspaper printing house will throw away the ends of rolls after every print run and they are usually happy for you to collect them (see Sources of materials on page 155).

Entrances

First impressions are often the strongest. So what you decide to place at the entrance to the classroom or studio will give a message about what is to come. Get this right and you are on the way to engaging the interest of your students.

In this section we will look at how you can make a simple statement before the session actually begins. We will look at ideas for dressing doorways, creating tunnels or passageways and how we can use a gazebo to quickly create an impression of excitement, mystery or intrigue.

Entrances I

Doorways

Doorways hold a promise of things to come. So let's look at what we can do to make them as interesting as possible. That way our session gets off to the best possible start.

Suspending something above the doorway, or putting a notice on the door is an excellent way of indicating that something different is going to happen. By using the two cup hooks above the door described in Structures 2, page 12, you can quickly give a visual clue that this lesson is drama, or storytelling, or art and craft etc.

Examples of how to increase the interest of the existing doorway:

- If a Musical Forest is planned (page 27) then some small instruments on strings that rattle or chime as students push them aside will set the scene. This is particularly useful to include if you have some visually impaired students as they will hear a clear auditory clue to indicate that they are entering the space.
- If the classroom has been turned into a Rainforest Jungle (page 47) then some of the same materials used in the environment suspended across the opening of the door on a baton held between the two hooks will give a foretaste of what is to come. Students will also get the tactile experience of pushing through the undergrowth as they enter.
- For the Snow Queen environment (page 97) hanging some ice blue and shiny silver material round the doorway will give the impression of entering through an ice doorway.
- If you have created an earth pit and are going to plant, or have already planted, herbs (page 137) then hanging some sprigs of thyme and rosemary beside the door anticipates the activity with the scent of the herbs.

- A notice on the door such as 'ENTER AT YOUR OWN RISK' or 'TREAD VERY CAREFULLY' will add tension. For non-readers a symbol with similar warnings will do the same job.

Entrances 2

Tunnels

A tunnel can be used as the entrance to the room and is in a sense simply an extended version of the doorway. What a tunnel does is delay the moment of entry into the space, which invests whatever is to come, with a little bit of intrigue and additional interest. This is particularly the case when the tunnel has a bend in it so that it is not possible to see where the tunnel ends from the point of entry.

Examples of how to create a simple tunnel:

- Place two poles (Structures 3, page 12) inside the door and 2 or 3 metres from it. Tie a line from each pole back to the door frame. Then hang a sheet of fabric from each line. Attach the corners of a third piece of fabric to the tops of each door post and the top of the poles to create a roof. You have now created a sense of passing through a tunnel. How much you add to this basic structure will depend on what your intention is.
- Maybe the quickest tunnel of all is created by using a classroom table draped with fabric placed in the doorway. In this way you can quickly and simply introduce a challenging way to enter the room. If you want whatever is inside the room screened from the participants until they get through the tunnel then you may need to screen

Figure 7 Crawling through tunnels of straw bales is a hard-to-resist activity.

off the gap above the table. One way of doing this is to suspend fabric from the lintel of the door down as far as the top of the table.

- Bales of straw can be configured to make a narrow tunnel that students love clambering through. It can leave a bit of a mess of straw but this is soon swept up and the multi-sensory nature of the straw can be worth the effort.

Entrances 3

Passageways

The passageway serves a similar purpose to the tunnel (Entrances 2, page 19) in that it can help us to create intrigue by delaying the students' entry into the space. Intrigue is enhanced if we create a bend in the passage so that when we guide the participants into the passageway the space they are heading towards is obscured from sight. The width of the passage will be determined by whether you have wheelchair users and the challenge you want to give your students. A narrower tunnel might be more daunting or challenging to enter than a wider one for some students.

Examples of how to create a passageway to enter through:

- By using rolls of corrugated card (Defining the space 1, page 15) we can create a passageway quickly and easily through which our group can enter. By using two lengths of 2 metre wide rolls side by side you can create an enclosed passageway that cannot be seen over. This idea is developed in Chapter 12 for the trenches of World War I.
- Use several free standing poles (Defining the space 2, page 16) with rope between them and hang fabric down from the rope. This will create a soft-sided passageway through which to enter. The fabric can be wafted by fans to enhance the kinaesthetic experience of coming into the space.
- A passageway can be created without sides too. This can be more appropriate for timid groups who like to see what they are letting themselves in for before proceeding. This is better described as a marked route rather than an actual passageway, but serves a similar purpose of guiding students into the space. The sides of the passage can be marked on the floor with chalk or by placing ropes to indicate the route to take.

Entrances 4

Gazebos

Putting up a gazebo is a quick, easy and cheap way of creating a basic structure for an entrance.* By discarding the plastic cover that usually comes with the gazebo you can personalise it and create the kind of space you want. This can be done by making an alternative cover out of coloured materials or by putting a net over it.

---

* The gazebo can be used as the structure to hang elements of several of the multi-sensory environments such as: Chapter 1, Musical Forest; Chapter 3, Undersea World; or Chapter 4, Rainforest Jungle.

Alternatively you can use the structure without a cover and hang things down the sides from the horizontal aluminium poles. This creates the impression of a large tent and participants can push the hangings aside to enter the space.

If the gazebo is too high for the available height in your classroom then you can leave the bottom section of the legs off – this may make it difficult for the larger wheelchair user to access it but you would be able to have students on cushions and mats on the floor.

A tip for making a gazebo quicker to erect on subsequent occasions is to colour-code the lengths of aluminium when it is first put up with paint or different coloured electrician's tape.

Environments and activities

Part 1

Rooms within rooms

Chapter 1

Musical Forest

The Musical Forest is suitable for either setting up before the students enter or for involving them in helping to set it up.

What is set up as your students enter the room

At the start The room is filled with a forest of trees suspended from the ceiling. The trees make musical chiming sounds when moved. The forest is made up of a series of cardboard tubes, decorated to look like trees. The Musical Forest makes an intriguing environment to explore during a drama or movement session or as an art installation in its own right.

An alternative is to completely make the environment during an art session with the students (and staff) before hanging it up to use as an installation or a setting for drama. In which case the students enter to find all the materials (below) laid out.

Different sensory channels

Visual
- different coloured materials on the trees;
- positioning of the trees – spaced out or close together;
- a light shining from behind the hanging trees – this can be a stage lantern, a simple domestic light or torch.

Auditory
- the sound of the copper pipes striking each other as the tree trunks are moved. The sound will be amplified by the carpet tube;
- small instruments such as bells attached to the trees;
- other objects that have percussive qualities tied onto trees;
- birdsong from a CD of sound effects.

Kinaesthetic
- different textured fabrics, paper – shiny, matt etc. – on the trees;
- crunch of woodchip on the floor.

Olfactory/ gustatory
- smell of woodchip;
- scent of any additions to the trees or woodchip, e.g. herbs.

Equipment needed

How much equipment you need will depend on how complex you want to make the environment. If it is being erected for a short time you might decide just to put up a few trees. If it is going to be in situ for a couple of weeks or a whole term then it may well be worth the time and trouble to create a whole forest.

The basic environment	• camouflage net to suspend across the ceiling from which the cardboard tubes can hang; • ropes to string across the room; • cardboard tubes from the inside of rolls of carpet – most carpet shops will gladly give these away; • copper pipes in a variety of lengths 10–30 cms. Plumbers throw lots of these away. As plumbers move to using more plastic we will need to find alternatives such as aluminium tent pegs; • wire; • string; • sharp, pointed instrument to make holes in cardboard tubes.
Visual	• different coloured paper or torn up magazine pictures for sticking onto the tubes; • shiny foils; • cellophane; • PVA Glue or Pritt stick for sticking paper to tubes; • light source – stage light, domestic lamp, torch.
Auditory	• small percussion instruments – e.g. bells, small rattles; • small percussive objects that make a noise when moved – e.g. bunch of keys, plastic bottle with beads in – these can be attached to the trees; • CD of sound effects, e.g. birdsong; • CD player.
Kinaesthetic	• different textured fabrics to stick or tie onto tubes; • strings and other fibrous materials to give the trees a textured bark and leaves; • collection of nuts or other hoarded items for squirrel puppet.
Olfactory/ gustatory	• scent in some form – essential oils – spray perfume; • herbs – to put onto the trees; • bag of woodchip to scatter beneath the trees to give texture underfoot as well as smell.
For using puppet and/ or character	• squirrel or other animal puppet; • a character. Basic costume – any one of jacket, cloak, scarf worn by the person playing the role will give a clear statement of character. A complete costume can be used but is by no means necessary.

Figure 8
Playing a role does not need a full costume. Here a pith helmet and jacket with binoculars create a hunter while a headscarf and waistcoat indicate a pirate.

How to put it together

1. Collect the materials you need from the above list – you may not need all of them – it will depend on what your purpose is.
2. Suspend the camouflage net or ropes to the fixing points above the space (Structures 1, page 11) that is to become the forest.
3. Make four holes at the top of each of the cardboard carpet (or other) tubes at north, south, east and west. See Figure 9 below.

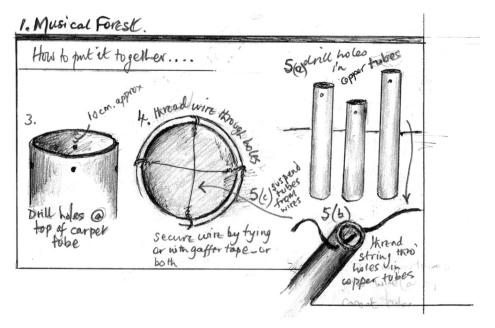

Figure 9 How to suspend copper tubes inside carpet tube 'trees' to make the sound for the Musical Forest.

4. Thread wire through the holes and across the tube from north to south and bend it down onto the side of the tube and gaffer tape the wire into position. Then do the same from east to west so you have a cross of wire across the carpet tube 10 cms or so from the end. From this the copper pipes, or other metal tubes can be suspended.
5. Using a drill bit suitable for metal, drill two holes at either side of one end of each of the copper pipes. Thread the string through the resulting holes and loop three or four lengths of copper over the crossed wires in place at the end of the cardboard tube so that the copper pipes are suspended inside the cardboard tubes.
6. Then hang the cardboard tubes, which now become the trees, from the ceiling. Thread strong string through the north and south holes in the carpet tube to attach to fixtures in the ceiling.

How long the tubes are will be partly determined by how high the ceiling is and how they are to be suspended. Long carpet tubes are quite a weight and will not easily be held by a string stretched across the ceiling. One solution is to use smaller tubes such as insides of rolls of baking foil and thinner copper tubes or aluminium tent pegs for the chime bars.

Ways to make use of the Musical Forest

Explore
environment

Use as an installation – and explore the musical forest
Students move among the tubes – either walking or in their chairs.★
When the carpet tubes are pushed the copper pipes will hit each other
and chime. The sound will be amplified by the carpet tube. They can:

- look at the colours on trees;
- feel and listen to the crunch of woodchip under feet;
- listen to the sounds;
- feel the textures on the trees and handle the woodchip – this can be
  lifted up on trays or in baskets for any wheelchair users to
  experience;
- smell the woodchip and any herbs attached to trees or spread on
  floor.

P Level 2(i) – Pupils react to new activities and experiences

**P Level 2(ii) – Pupils cooperate with shared exploration and supported
participation**

Speaking – P Level 4 – Pupils communicate about events and feelings

Puppetry

**Introduce an animal puppet – such as a squirrel or tiger – into
the forest**
Which way you choose to introduce the puppet will depend on your
group.

- Students could come across the puppet as they explore the forest –
  this might be more fun and more of a surprise. It has the potential
  to be challenging to manage.
- Students sit in a group facing the forest. The squirrel appears out of
  the trees and approaches them. It is nervous at first approach.
  Students find ways of gaining its confidence. Each student has time
  to get close to the squirrel – feel its fur etc. The squirrel can
  become playful and steal things and run off into the forest to hide
  them. The benefits of this will be enhanced by taking lots of time
  for the meetings.
- The squirrel has a problem – it has lost its stash of nuts and needs
  students to help to find it in the forest. The nuts can be hidden
  throughout the forest before the start of the session. The students
  go one by one to search for it and then return to the group and the
  squirrel to report on what they have seen or found; or to bring
  back any nuts they have found.

★ If you are working with wheelchair users then cutting down the length of some of the tubes
enables the bottom of the tube to be level with the head of someone sitting in a wheelchair. This
enables them to be able to listen more easily to the resonance of the chimes down the tubes.

Figure 10 Puppets have the capacity to command complete attention.

Speaking – P Level 4 – Pupils repeat, copy and imitate between 10 and 50 single words or phrases or use a repertoire of objects of reference or symbols

Meet a character

Introduce a character – a woman in shabby clothing
As for the squirrel above, the woman can be discovered in the forest or can come out of it. The woman has a problem. The problem you decide on will depend upon the age and abilities of the group. Possibilities include:

- She is lost – can the students help her find the path? The students go into the forest to see if they can locate a path. If they find one they guide her to it and she thanks them and goes on her way.
- She has lost something – her pet cat, her child, her purse, something precious? The students help search the forest and find what is missing.

- She is hungry and needs some food and water – the students supply her needs. They could draw the food on paper as a representation of it/they could get her real water, or pretend water in a real cup.

Speaking – P Level 6 – Pupils ask simple questions to obtain information

Numeracy   Simple counting – keep a tally of the nuts as they are brought back out of the forest for the squirrel, count trees, measure which is nearest floor etc.

Number – P Level 5 – Pupils demonstrate an understanding of one to one correspondence in a range of contexts

Art and craft   **Use as an art activity and visual display**
This idea can be used as an art project in which the students decorate the carpet tubes to make them realistically represent trees before the forest is put in place. You can use paint, tissue paper, cellophane, ribbon and many other materials.

Musical Forest in action

One example of how this environment has been used

In this example of the Musical Forest the music is made in a different way to that described above.

Hanging strips of fabric are set up before the students enter. Green fabric is suspended around the forest to enclose the space and make it more intimate. Some of the strips of fabric have small metallic objects and small musical instruments (bells, rattles etc.) tied on to provide the musical and percussive sounds when the fabric is moved.

Students then took turns to move through the hangings and interact with any of them in any way that they like. We allow them to touch or not touch as they please so that decision making is passed over to the student.

Then the students sat – most of them in wheelchairs – in a semi-circle facing the forest. A pelican puppet pushed its way slowly through the forest. The puppeteer focussed the attention of the puppet entirely on the forest. It was busy in its own world, minding its own business, as it were. We want to give the message that there are no expectations on the students to interact in any way. We are not trying to get the students to take notice of it or to interact with it or to do anything – the pelican is just there.

After a while the pelican came out of the forest and noticed the students. It was very timid and kept its distance at first; going back among the trees to hide and peer out. All this was designed to build up curiosity and not to rush any potential interest and interactions. Again the message is that we, or rather the pelican, are not trying to get a response. It is fine simply to sit and watch, it is fine to reach out or not and it is fine to seek a more committed interaction. In due course some of the students interacted with the pelican as it became increasingly confident and playful, eventually getting up to mischief such as untying shoelaces and stealing cups which it had taken into the forest to hide.

When the pelican had left, the students went into the forest to recover what had been stolen.

Suggested learning outcomes

PMLD/SLD	P Level 2(i) – Pupils react to new activities and experiences
	P Level 2(ii) – Pupils cooperate with shared exploration and supported participation
	Speaking – P Level 4 – Pupils communicate about events and feelings
	Speaking – P Level 4 – Pupils repeat, copy and imitate between 10 and 50 single words or phrases or use a repertoire of objects of reference or symbols
	Speaking – P Level 6 – Pupils ask simple questions to obtain information
	Number – P Level 5 – Pupils demonstrate an understanding of one to one correspondence in a range of contexts

Chapter 2

Storytelling Sari Tent

The Storytelling Sari Tent is not suitable for students to put up.

The environment described here is a blank canvas for whatever story you are going to tell or activity you are going to involve your students in. Your intended use will determine what, and how much, you add to the environment.

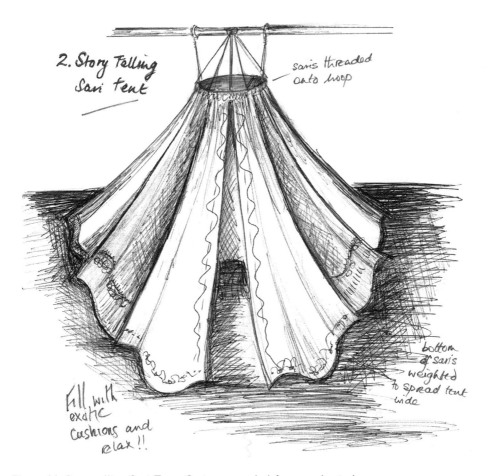

Figure 11 Storytelling Sari Tent. Saris suspended from a plastic hoop.

What is set up as your students enter the room

At the start   At the centre of the room is the tent made up of colourful saris suspended from the ceiling. They are spread out in the manner of a tepee to accommodate the whole of the group. Two of the saris are pulled back to provide an entrance.

The room is dimly lit and background music plays as the students enter.

The students enter the sari tent and settle down in their wheelchairs, on beanbags, floor mats or whatever is appropriate.

Different sensory channels

Visual
- colourful saris with a variety of texture and colours;
- small light bulbs (such as fairy lights); or
- imitation candles in paper lanterns hung from the centre of the tent.

Auditory
- the voice of the storyteller;
- the music to be played in the background;
- any sound effects to accompany the story;
- microphone and amplifier.

Kinaesthetic
- cushions, soft mats, beanbags or duvets on the floor of the tent for students and staff to sit on. These make a comfortable and cosy space;
- objects relevant to the story (chosen according to the age of the students, theme and characters of the story).

Olfactory/gustatory
- fruits for tasting (if the plot of the story allows), placed in baskets around the floor beside the floor cushions;
- scent from oriental perfume oils.

Equipment needed

How much equipment you need will depend on how complex you want to make the environment. If it is being put up for a short time you might decide just to include the hanging saris. If it is going to be in situ for a couple of weeks or a whole term then it may well be worth the time and trouble to add in some of the other elements too.

The basic environment
- saris – plain or printed according to what you have available, your purposes and the plot of the story. If plain then theme colours could be used. The saris are suspended from the ceiling to make a tent;
- methods of hanging saris: broom handles or a plastic hoop – see below;
- gaffer tape;
- safety pins to pin together the side-ends of saris so that no gaps appear.

Visual
- fairy lights;
- paper lamps and imitation candles – battery operated;
- props, pictures, puppets etc., relevant to the story/activity;
- a directional light such as an angle poise to focus attention on an object or puppet – see below;
- a special storytelling chair helps to raise the status of the activity.

Auditory
- CD player;
- music CD with the appropriate recordings;
- sound effects CD of the sounds from the story to be told.

Kinaesthetic
- cushions, chairs or mats;
- objects according to the theme and characters in the story.

Olfactory/
gustatory
- fruit or other foods if it is to be a tasting activity or the story includes sharing of food;
- perfume oils in containers.

How to put it together

1. Collect the materials you need from the above list. You may not need all of them: it will depend on what your purpose is.
2. Suspend the saris in one of the four methods below:
   (a) Attach lengths of string to the two corners at one end of each sari and then tie them up to any available fixing points on the ceiling, making them into as close a circle as fixings allow. This method may be the most suitable in a classroom with limited height.
   (b) Each of the saris is sewn along one end to make a tube. A broom handle (with a hole drilled in each end) is then passed through the tube and a string is threaded through each of the two holes in the broom handle to suspend it from the ceiling. You then hang as many saris as you need from your fixtures on the ceiling to enclose a space.
   (c) Hang the saris from a large hoop. For this you need height so the hall may be the best place. The plastic hoops that are common in schools' PE cupboards are ideal. Cut through the hoop, or pull it apart if the join is loose enough, to enable the saris to be threaded onto it. Thread the hoop through the tube at the end of each sari – as many as you need – and then rejoin the hoop with gaffer tape (it makes it stronger if you insert a piece of dowel inside the hoop before taping it back together). Then suspend the hoop from the ceiling. This method gives a narrow top to the tent but the bottom of the saris can be spread out as far as is necessary to accommodate the size of group. See Figure 11 above.
   (d) A fourth method of creating the sari tent is to use a gazebo (Entrances 4, page 20) and suspend saris over the frame from the apex of the gazebo down each side. The size of the tent can be increased by pulling the saris away from the base of the gazebo to accommodate a larger group.

For all four of these methods the saris can be pinned together with safety pins if you don't want gaps to appear between each sari.

3. Introduce the chairs, cushions, mats or duvets.
4. Put any lighting in position.
5. Place any objects, food or materials relating to the story or activity to come.
6. Set up the music system – CD player.
7. Set up microphone and amplifier.
8. Position the storytelling chair if using.

Ways to make use of the Storytelling Sari Tent

Explore
environment

Explore the tent

This could happen as a way of students becoming comfortable with the space before the story begins. It is the sort of activity that can be lingered over and it might be worth taking the time to hoist students out of their chairs so that they can experience whatever is in the tent from supporting floor cushions. The students enter the tent one by one. They can then:

- feel the textures of cushions;
- listen to the sounds of the music;
- smell the perfume oils;
- notice changes in the lighting effects;
- handle objects.

P Level P1 (i)/(ii) – Pupils encounter/show emerging awareness of activities and experiences

Puppetry

Introduce a puppet

This could be a character that occurs in the story. It can give students a tactile and visual experience of the character in the story if they find it difficult to focus on the verbal narration.

It is helpful to leave lengthy pauses in the narrative so that the puppet has time to interact with each student during the story.

Create a heightened effect

Change the lighting to allow the light to be directed onto the story-telling chair or the puppet as the action shifts from one to the other.

Listening – P Level 4 – Pupils respond appropriately to simple requests which contain one key word, sign or symbol

Make
soundscapes

We have found that non-verbal students often vocalise when relaxed in such a space as this. Have a microphone on a lead attached to an amplifier to hand – then if one of the students does begin to vocalise you can bring the microphone to them and they can hear their own voice over the speakers.

P Level 3(i) – Pupils begin to communicate intentionally

Storytelling

Tell a story

The setting is suitable for the telling of almost any story. Ones that work well are those that have within them lots of multi-sensory elements.

Either use the storytelling chair or the storyteller can move round among the students.

Listening – P Level 7 – Pupils listen, attend to and follow stories for short stretches of time

Tasting   The story tent is a relaxing environment for tasting food. Some stories may have food built into them – but if they don't we can add it anyway – a kind of food additive! The heroine could stop by the road for something to eat, or the warriors could break from their preparations to feast before battle.

Prepared food could be tasted by the students while there is a pause in the storytelling. Soft fruit works well – particularly during the summer when it is in season and tastes better. Even some tube-fed students are able to experience flavour on their lips.

Speaking – P Level 4 – Pupils communicate about events and feelings

Sari Tent in action

One example of how this environment has been used

For this example of the Sari Tent in action we replaced the colourful saris with a white parachute as we wanted it to represent the inside of a whale's belly for a story about the sea. We were working in a theatre studio with five children, who all had profound and multiple learning difficulties, and their parents. We used a loose narrative to bring together a number of sea-related multi-sensory experiences over a period of three days.

To create the whale's belly we suspended the parachute using method 2(c) in the 'How to put it together' section above (page 37). Inside the parachute we hung strips of red fabric and lengths of wide red elastic tape that we found in a recycling depot. The red against the white parachute gave a strong visual contrast for the V.I. students as well as representing the blood of the whale. Some of the lengths of elastic and fabric hung down far enough for the students to be able to reach them while lying on the floor.

The tent was filled with beanbags and cushions. A recording of the sound of the sea played quietly in the background.

In order to enter the whale's belly each child was hoisted out of his chair and placed on a large beanbag which was on a low trolley with wheels. Then with a vocalist making whale-like noises over a microphone the child, sometimes with parent on the trolley as well to give support, was pulled over the sea and through the whale's mouth (part of the parachute was held up to allow entry) into its belly.

When all the students were sitting or lying comfortably with their parents on the beanbags inside the belly we allowed a period of calm relaxation with low light and just the constant sound of the sea. The vocalist, sitting among the students in the tent, then re-introduced the whale-like sounds over the microphone. This prompted some of the students to vocalise so we passed the microphone round to them so that all could hear their own vocalisations amplified through the sound system.

Suggested learning outcomes

P Level P1 (i)/(ii) – Pupils encounter/show emerging awareness of activities and experiences

Listening – P Level 4 – Pupils respond appropriately to simple requests which contain one key word, sign or symbol

P Level 3(i) – Pupils begin to communicate intentionally

Listening – P Level 7 – Pupils listen, attend to and follow stories for short stretches of time

Speaking – P Level 4 – Pupils communicate about events and feelings

Chapter 3

Undersea World

The Undersea World is suitable for either setting up before the students enter or involving the students in helping to make the fish beforehand and setting up the Undersea World environment.

What is set up as your students enter the room

At the start The students enter the room to find the walls draped with fabric – greens and blues – the colours of the sea. Sea creatures hang down from a blue camouflage net that is suspended from the ceiling – fish of different shapes and phosphorescent colour, octopuses, pieces of coral, seaweed etc. Lights reflect from the hanging shapes.

The sea floor is scattered with sand and a collection of rounded ocean pebbles and shells are piled in one corner.

The sound of the sea pulsates.

In baskets on the floor and on tables are cardboard cut-out shapes of fish and sea creatures and materials with which to decorate them.

Students are invited to sit on mats and cushions surrounding the sea.

Alternative ways to create the initial effect
Use a gazebo for a smaller space instead of the whole room. This will allow you to hang the drapes from the sides of the gazebo and the fish etc. can be suspended from the cross struts.

Whichever method you use the idea is to create a very different environment from that to which they are accustomed. This gives the message that something different, something exciting is about to happen.

Different sensory channels

Visual
- different shades of blues and green fabric hanging from walls. Any other sea colours can be included of course. However, restricting the palette can be more effective;
- brightly coloured materials for sea creatures that provide a contrast to the palette of the sea colours;

- reflective papers and foils stuck on fish, coral etc. and hanging with seaweed to catch the light;
- lighting effects – stage lighting if available, a limited amount of the ceiling lights or a free standing domestic lamp. Having a low light in the room creates a dramatic atmosphere;
- a simple domestic light shining onto some of the fish can give a dramatic effect and be directed to where individual students can access its effect;
- props such as the baskets with the parts of the fish or sea creatures;
- different shapes of sea creature.

Auditory
- sound of the voice of the storyteller;
- music if played;
- recorded sounds of the sea.

Kinaesthetic
- different textures on the hanging fabrics and sea creatures;
- a variety of textured paper or tissue;
- sand and pebbles on floor;
- shells with a variety of shapes and textures;
- soft floor mat and cushions.

Olfactory/ gustatory
- scent of the sea from shells and seaweed if they have been recently collected from the beach.

Equipment needed

How much equipment you need will depend on how complex you want to make the environment. If it is being put up for a short time you might want to create a small scene with a backdrop of one blue drape. If it is going to be in situ for a couple of weeks or a whole term then it may well be worth the time and trouble to create the Undersea World with the whole room covered.

The basic environment
- blue/green drapes to cover walls;
- blue camouflage net to suspend across the ceiling from which the undersea creatures can hang from elastic strings;
- stage lights to give blue/green sea effects.

Visual
- plastic colanders to hang upside down with tissue suspended from them (octopuses or jelly fish);
- cut-out shapes of fish from bubble wrap;
- baking foil, coloured foil-backed paper, cellophane, lighting gel, shiny card with holographic designs, to cut out shapes for scales;
- tissue in different colours
- sequins for texture and to reflect light;
- torn-up plastic bags for seaweed;
- glue for decorating sea creatures;
- phosphorescent pens to make fish glow under ultra violet light;
- ultra violet light source if using.

Auditory
- CD player;
- CDs of sound effects of the sea.

Kinaesthetic	• different textured paper, cellophane or tissue;
	• bubble wrap;
	• string – different textures;
	• plastic bags, string and other fibrous materials to make seaweed.
Olfactory/ gustatory	• smell of seaweed and shells if recently collected from beach;
	• scent in some other form – essential oils or spray perfume – to put onto sea creatures.

How to put it together

1. Collect the materials you need from the above list – you may not need all of them – it will depend on what your purpose is.
2. Suspend the camouflage net or ropes to fixing points above the space.
3. Hang the fish and other sea creatures from the elastic strings that drop down from the net hanging above. How you suspend the fish etc. depends on the effect you want to create and how you intend to use the environment created.
   (a) If it is part of a story you may want the fish to be swimming at low enough level for the students to walk among or move in wheelchairs between them.
   (b) If it is for a group of students with complex and profound needs it may be that they will experience it lying on mats on the floor so the fish will need to be near ground level.
   (c) If the Undersea World is going to be left up for some time it may be better to have the fish suspended high enough so that everyone can still get around the classroom.
   (d) It is useful to be able to raise and lower the Undersea World so that it can be experienced by walking through it and then lowered for students using wheelchairs and then again to be accessed by students lying on the floor. This can be achieved if you have in place the pulley system with cleats on the wall. (Structures 1, page 11.)
4. Put chairs, cushions and/or mats in place.
5. Adjust lighting in the room. Dim lights will create a more mysterious atmosphere if that is what you want.
6. Consider creating a position that a storyteller can take up within the environment if you intend to use one. For example a stool concealed as a rock would be a good place for a person to sit.

Ways to make use of the Undersea World

Explore environment	• look at the fish/seaweed etc.;
	• feel the textures of fish/seaweed etc. with hands or as they drape across faces;
	• handle sand, pebbles and shells;
	• listen to the sounds of the sea while among the creatures.

P Level P1(i)/(ii) – Pupils encounter activities and experiences

Puppetry	• animate the cut-out fish; • use one of the fish as the subject of a story such as *The Rainbow Fish*. Suspend it from two threads (one attached to the head and one to the tail) in the manner of a simple marionette with the threads attached to a stick that is used to manipulate the puppet. The puppet can then be passed round among the students as the story is told.
Storytelling	The space can be used as a setting for a sea-related story. This could be told or read by the teacher.

Listening – P Level 7 – Pupils listen and attend to stories

Numeracy	• simple counting of creatures, pebbles and shells; • collecting creatures into categories – the fish with anything shiny on them, those with blue, etc.

Maths Using and Applying – P Level 6 – Pupils sort objects to given criteria

Literacy	Make up a collective story about the fish and the other elements of the environment which the teacher or one of the students writes down as students come up with ideas.

Speaking – P Level 7 – Pupils contribute appropriately one to one and in small group discussions

Art activities	The type of art activity will depend of course upon the dexterity of your students. The idea of having the Undersea World can be used as an art project in which the students can design and make sea creatures to hang in the environment. Students with sufficient dexterity can be invited to make the fish that then become the Undersea World creatures ready to hang from the ceiling and the walls. The creatures can include fish, octopus, coral reef and seaweeds and anything else that relates to the story to be told.

Undersea World in action

One example of how this environment has been used

This example is from a residency in which we used the story *The Rainbow Fish* by Marcus Pfister. See Figure 12 below. The students with their carers and parents made fish using different coloured shiny card for the scales and bubble wrap to stuff the body of the fish. The fish were then suspended with a length of fishing wire from the head and one from the tail attached to a short rod so that they could be held as a marionette might be. The

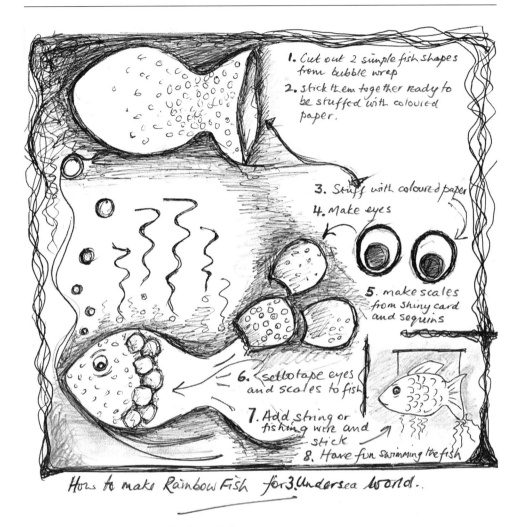

1. Cut out 2 simple fish shapes from bubble wrap

2. Stick them together ready to be stuffed with coloured paper.

3. Stuff with coloured paper

4. Make eyes

5. make scales from shiny card and sequins

6. sellotape eyes and scales to fish

7. Add string or fishing wire and stick

8. Have fun swimming the fish

How to make Rainbow Fish for 3. Undersea World.

Figure 12 How to make a Rainbow Fish.

fish then 'swam' around the students in a kind of dance, the shiny card catching the light. We suspended a blue camouflage net above the space and one by one each student came forward and was invited to choose where she would like her fish to be suspended. This created an undersea environment of swimming fish through which the students passed in their wheelchairs on a journey to look for friends for the Rainbow Fish.

In this way we were able to give the students responsibility for creating part of the environment – helping to make the fish and deciding where they should hang – in which they then experienced elements of the story.

Suggested learning outcomes

P Level P1(i)/(ii) – Pupils encounter activities and experiences

Listening – P Level 7 – Pupils listen and attend to stories

Maths Using and Applying – P Level 6 – Pupils sort objects to given criteria

Speaking – P Level 7 – Pupils contribute appropriately one to one and in small group discussions

Chapter 4

Rainforest Jungle

This environment is very suitable for involving the students in helping to make the elements of the jungle and to help set it up.

What is set up as your students enter the room

At the start   The students wait outside the door. From inside come the sounds of the rainforest – a monkey chatters, parrots scream, rain pours down in torrents. Anticipation builds as the sounds fade and the teacher slowly opens the door.

The students enter.

In front of them – hanging from the ceiling – is a thick tangle of vines and creepers, some with foliage, others more like bare ropes. Some reach the floor, others are shorter. Leaves of various sizes and different shades of green are interspersed with brilliant red and yellow tropical flowers. The students gather in front of the jungle.

The sound of running water from a water pump and pond.

Among the trees some movement. Something is approaching . . . a monkey? A person . . . ?

Different sensory channels

Visual
- many different shades of green and brown;
- bright and contrasting coloured tropical flowers;
- reflective papers and foils to catch the light;
- lighting effects – stage lighting if available, domestic angle poise, or changing the existing ceiling lights – covering windows or uncovering them.

Auditory
- monkeys screeching, parrots screaming, other jungle noises on a recording;
- sound of dripping water from a garden pond fountain in a container – tin bath or bucket; or
- the recording of a running stream.

Figure 13 Here the impression of a jungle is created by strips of material hanging from a camouflage net. Low-level stage lighting adds to the atmosphere. Having stage lighting and being able to black out a room gives opportunities for many effects but it is also possible to create different lighting effects with simple domestic lamps.

Figure 14
A boy takes notice of the light source as he moves through the jungle made from fabric suspended from a camouflage net.

| Kinaesthetic | • different textured fabrics hanging down will allow a variety of touching experiences as students progress through the hanging jungle;
• woodchip on the floor (can be useful to put plastic down to protect the floor and to facilitate collecting up the woodchip at the end of the activity) gives a different feel when walked on or when chair wheels move across it;
• bare feet on the woodchip;
• spraying students with a fine spray of water – some love this while others might be discomforted. |
| Olfactory/
gustatory | • woodchip on the floor gives a rich scent. Keeping it in the bag until just before use will maximise the depth of scent;
• artificial scent of tropical flowers. |

Equipment needed

How much equipment you need will depend on how complex you want to make the environment. If it is being put up for a short time you might decide just to go for some of the hangings. If it is going to be in situ for a couple of weeks or a whole term then it may well be worth the time and trouble to add in some of the other elements too.

The basic environment	• camouflage net; • means of hanging the net above the students (Structures 1, page 11 or Structures 3, page 12); • lengths of fabric of different textures; • string for tying camouflage net up; • pegs or magnets if students are likely to tug hard at the hangings; • plastic sheet to place under the woodchip and water feature.
Visual	• sugar paper and other sorts of paper for making large leaf shapes; • tissue paper for brightly coloured tropical flowers; • pipe cleaners or similar for flower stems.
Auditory	• recording of monkeys and parrots and other rainforest sound effects; • CD player.
Kinaesthetic	• cellophane and/or shiny paper for alternative textures for leaves; • water features; • spray bottles for water – the type used to spray plants with a fine spray through a nozzle work well; • tin bath or other receptacle for water. It needs to be big enough to accommodate the garden pump; • small garden water pump.
Olfactory/ gustatory	• scent in some form – essential oils, spray perfume, herbs – to put onto the flowers; • bag of woodchip to scatter and give texture and smells.
For drama idea/s	• monkey puppets – adult and young; • basic costume for character.

How to put it together

1. Collect the materials you need from the above list – you may not need all of them – it will depend on what your purpose is.
2. Suspend the camouflage net from hooks on walls or poles and bases. Tie the corners up first getting as much tension as possible so that the sag in the middle is minimised. Tying a string across the centre of the net will help with this as will tying it off from the side of the net to the side of the room. It can be useful, when hanging the camouflage net, to hang it in such a way that it can be raised and lowered to varying heights (Structures 1, page 11). This enables you to lower it so that children can access the forest while lying on mats on the floor and raise it so that the hanging material etc. does not get tangled in the wheels if the children are using wheelchairs.
3. Make the hangings that will become the rainforest trees and creepers:
    (a) Plaiting different coloured lengths of fabric together gives a richness to the creepers.
    (b) Use different textures of string, e.g. sisal, baler twine, or lengths of torn fabric to make a variety of hangings.
    (c) Make the brightly coloured tissue paper flowers.
    (d) Make the large tropical-type leaves cut from sugar paper, cellophane etc.
4. Tie the hangings and flowers onto the camouflage net to make the dense rainforest.
5. Position plastic sheet under water feature and woodchip.
6. Position whatever you are using for a pond and fill it with water and put the pump in position. The depth of the water will need to be sufficient to cover the pump.
7. Scatter woodchip.

Ways to make use of the Rainforest Jungle

Explore environment

Explore the rainforest
*   look at the creepers and vines;
*   feel the textures of leaves and vines with hands or as they drape across faces when pushing through the undergrowth;
*   look at, touch and smell the flowers;
*   listen to the sounds of the jungle while among the trees;
*   listen to running water from pump;
*   put hands into the pool;
*   feel the 'rain' from water spray bottles;
*   dip hands into the water of the pond.

Also see Chapter 18, Garden Pond for other pond activities.

P Level 2(ii) – Pupils cooperate with shared exploration and supported participation

Puppetry

Introduce a puppet – such as a monkey – into the jungle
*   students could come across the monkey as they explore the jungle;
*   students could sit in a group facing the jungle: the monkey appears out of the trees and approaches them. It is nervous at first approach.

Students find ways of gaining its confidence. Each student has time to get close to the monkey and feel its fur. The monkey can become playful and untie shoelaces and steal things and run off into the jungle;

• the monkey has a problem: it has lost its young and needs student help to find it in the forest. The students go one by one to search for it and then return to the group and the monkey to report on what they have seen on their journey through the jungle.

Speaking – P Level 8 – To take part in role play with confidence

Meet a
character

Introduce a character – a woman in shabby clothing

• as for the monkey, the woman can be discovered in the jungle or can come out of it;

• the woman has a problem. The problem you decide on will depend upon the age and abilities of the group. A couple of examples:
  – she is lost: can the students help her find the path? The students go into the jungle to see if they can locate a path – if so they guide her to it and she thanks them and goes on her way;
  – she has lost something: her pet monkey, her child, her purse, something precious. The students help search the jungle and find what is missing.

Listening – P Level 4 – Pupils respond appropriately to simple requests which contain one key word

Literacy

Retell the story that emerged from the monkey puppet or woman in shabby clothing above, for example:
1. We saw the monkey hiding in the jungle.
2. We followed it and stroked it.
3. We made friends with it etc.

Speaking – P Level 6 – Pupils initiate and maintain short conversations

Numeracy

Comparison – who can find the longest creeper?
Number – how many pink flowers are there?
Measurement – how far is it from the front to the back of the jungle?

Maths Shape, Space and Measure – P Level 5 – Pupils compare the overall size of one object where there is a marked difference

Art and craft   1. Make tropical flowers. Cut circles of tissue paper – a variety of bright colours and sizes. Lay several on top of each other and make a small hole in the centre of each. Thread a pipe cleaner through the hole and secure the petals.

2. Make creepers. Plait string and bits of scrap fabric into lengths that can be hung from the ceiling. A variety of textures will give a rich experience.

Rainforest Jungle in action

One example of how this environment has been used

We are in a special school hall that has been transformed into a theatre studio with black-out and stage lighting. The students, 20 of them, have a variety of learning difficulties, mostly higher level SLD with some ASD and a couple of PMLD, most have some spoken language. The week-long residency involves the students creating a narrative about a woman they have met at the beginning of the week who has a dilemma and who becomes the protagonist of the story. Part of this process involves the students making decisions about the kind of landscapes through which the protagonist will travel on her journey and what dangers she will encounter. They decide that one of the landscapes is to be a jungle in which they – the woman and the students (they have been recruited to help her on her journey) – will encounter a dangerous man. They will have to find a way to get past him.

The students spend a morning creating the jungle and they also decide to make a costume for the dangerous man. In the afternoon they come into the space with the protagonist woman to find the man in place among their jungle – blocking their path. They are given the task of coming up with a plan to get past the man. In groups of five they spend time deciding – some plan stealth, to creep through the jungle so that he doesn't notice them – others decide to approach the man and attempt persuasion or trickery.

Their plans are then put into practice, each group enacting their own idea while the others watch. They are successful and they continue their journey with the woman.

This environment was not particularly like a rainforest jungle. This did not matter because our main purpose was to empower the students by giving them control over the environment in which they were working, rather than to create an authentic rainforest. Had it been important to get authenticity we could have spent more time researching – looked at pictures of the Amazon rainforest, for example, found video footage of people in a rainforest and then provided materials to enable us to represent more accurately what the environment would actually be like.

Suggested learning outcomes

PMLD/SLD	P Level 2(ii) – Pupils cooperate with shared exploration and supported participation
	Listening – P Level 4 – Pupils respond appropriately to simple requests which contain one key word
	Maths Shape, Space and Measure – P Level 5 – Pupils compare the overall size of one object where there is a marked difference
	Speaking – P Level 6 – Pupils initiate and maintain short conversations
	Speaking – P Level 8 – To take part in role play with confidence

Chapter 5

Clothes Rail Screens

This environment is suitable for involving the students in setting it up.

What is set up as your students enter the room

At the start   A number of clothes rails on wheels.

On the floor or on tables are baskets with materials for making the hangings that will go onto the clothes rails:
- fabrics of different colours and textures;
- musical instruments;
- objects with percussive qualities;
- herbs;
- anything else you and the students are minded to think of!

Different sensory channels

Visual
- different coloured fabrics;
- shapes of objects and materials.

Auditory
- sound of musical instruments and percussive objects;
- sound of wheeled screens moving.

Kinaesthetic
- textures of fabric and other materials;
- touch of musical instruments.

Olfactory/ gustatory
- herbs;
- lavender.

Equipment needed

How much equipment you need will depend on whether you are focussing just on one of the senses or creating a rail for each of the senses or indeed for another purpose.

The basic environment   Clothes rails on wheels – the sort that market traders use. How many you have might depend on your intention. Four or five, for example, allow you to enclose an area in a classroom or hall.

Visual	• different coloured fabrics; • coloured ribbons; • any other materials to suspend from rails.
Auditory	• small musical instruments; • objects that have percussive qualities; • different lengths of bamboo canes for tubular bells.
Kinaesthetic	• assortment of fabrics with different textures; • feathers.
Olfactory/ gustatory	• a selection of herbs – rosemary, sage, thyme; • lavender bags.

How to put it together

1. Collect the materials you need from the above list – you may not need all of them – it will depend which rails you intend to create.
2. Put the rails together.
3. Assemble the materials for each rail.
4. Suspend the materials by string or tape onto the top rail of the clothes rails.
5. If you want a more secure screen then tie off the hangings onto the bottom rail.
6. Wheel the resulting creations to wherever you want to use them.

Ways to make use of Clothes Rail Screens

Explore environment	• use sticks to play the percussion rails, or shake different instruments; • touch the different textures of rails hung with fabrics etc.; • smell the hanging herbs.

P Level 1–3 – As appropriate to pupil

Touring exhibition	This environment is ideal for moving around. Your class could make a rail and it could be taken round to other classes for visits. A number of them could become a multi-sensory exhibition for a school open day.
Make soundscapes	1. Students choose percussion instruments to hang along the clothes rail and then take turns in playing them. You could record what they play in order to keep a record of it or to accompany another activity at a later date. 2. Suspend a selection of percussive objects from the upper bar of the rails – small kitchen utensils, lengths of stick or bamboo, anything hard that makes a sound when hit. Then students 'play' the home-made percussion instrument with sticks.

Music – P Level 4 – Pupils are aware of cause and effect in familiar events, instruments are banged, shaken etc.

Screening a discrete space for work	By creating a number of screens you can encircle part of the room for other purposes – a drama, the telling of a story, or simply to do some numeracy with a difference.
Individual working alone but as part of a group activity	For some students (those on some parts of the autistic spectrum) working as part of a group is a challenge. Using a clothes rail allows an individual to work with a member of staff outside the classroom to create something on the rail that can then be brought back into the classroom to share with the rest of the group.
Numeracy	Students make a numeracy rail by tying different numbers of objects onto lengths of string. (1) washer; (2) flowers; (3) curtain rings, etc. The students then identify which number is which and suspend them in numerical order etc.

Maths Number – P Level 7 – Recognise numerals 1–5/Count at least five objects reliably

A magical doorway or screen	Create a Narnia-style wardrobe as a portal to another world. This is done by hanging fabric or rope down from the top rail and securing it to the bottom one. Students, or a teacher representing a character, can then push through the screen to arrive at another destination. Students can then pass through in order to be in the part of the room where a story is to be told. If you have any wheelchair users in your group you could leave off the bottom bar of the rail to allow the wheelchairs to pass through.

Clothes Rail Screen in action

One example of how this environment has been used

The mobility of the screens can be an asset as will be seen in this example where a student was enabled to take part in a group session when she would otherwise have been excluded in some way.

We were working with a group of 20 students in a theatre on a week-long project. The story that the students were devising included the creation of a haunted house in order to scare the villain in the story. For this activity the students worked in small groups and the purpose of each one was to create some part of the house that would scare the villain when he passed through. One girl, lets call her Carol, who is high on the autistic spectrum, was finding it very difficult to be part of this activity; she was distressed, running around the studio and clambering over the seating. A member of staff took Carol outside the space to allow her to calm down. They then worked together using a clothes rail and some fabric strips and percussion instruments and percussive objects to create a sound curtain that could be activated in the haunted house.

When all the groups in the studio had constructed their part of the haunted house Carol wheeled her sound curtain in and placed it in among the other haunted parts of the house. Carol stood beside it and activated the sounds when the villain passed by.

In this way Carol was able to be included as part of a group activity without having to stay in the room when it was too confusing and busy for her to feel comfortable.

Figure 15 A Clothes Rail Screen as used in Bamboozle's touring production of 'Crazy Hair'. This principle can be used in the classroom too. Lengths of fabric torn up and hung from the top rail in much the same way as the rope is used here will make an effective screen for hiding behind or entering through.

Figure 16
The clothes rail screen can be used to create an entrance that students can clamber through.

Suggested learning outcomes

P Level 1–3 – As appropriate to pupil

Music – P Level 4 – Pupils are aware of cause and effect in familiar events, instruments are banged, shaken etc.

Maths Number – P Level 7 – Recognise numerals 1–5/Count at least five objects reliably

Chapter 6

Laundry

The basic washing line part of this environment is very quick and easy to put up. The Laundry is most suitable for setting up before the students enter. However there is some scope for involving the students in helping to set up the washing lines beforehand.

What is set up as your students enter the room

At the start   Two or more washing lines are hanging across the classroom or hall. The lines intersect each other thus making a loosely enclosed space. They have clothes of different colours, sizes and textures hanging from them, but the lines are not full; there are gaps between the clothes. Beneath the washing lines are buckets with water in them and a large laundry basket with clothes spilling from it across the floor.

The students enter the room in pairs or groups of three. Each group is given a bag of clothes pegs as they enter. The students sit on mats or in chairs in a semi-circle facing the setting.

Music plays quietly.

Different sensory channels

Visual	• clothes of different colour, size and shape; • buckets, basket and clothes.
Auditory	• recorded music to play in the background; • sound of the wind; • sound of wind machine.
Kinaesthetic	• different textured fabrics for sensory exploration; • touch of metal buckets and wickerwork of the basket; • water of different temperature in the buckets; • bubbles, foam from the bubble mixture; • feel of the wind from wind machine or strong fans.
Olfactory/ gustatory	• scent of soap and washing powder.

Equipment needed

How much equipment you need will depend on how complex you want to make the environment. If it is being put up for a short time you might decide just to put up the washing lines. If it is going to be in situ for a couple of weeks or a whole term then it may well be worth the time and trouble to add in some of the other elements too.

The basic environment	• washing lines (or lengths of rope) to hang across the classroom or hall; • poles and bases if using to tie washing lines onto.
Visual	• clothes in a variety of shapes, sizes, colours and textures; • pegs; • bags for the pegs; • laundry basket – or any large basket/s if a laundry basket is not available; • bottles of bubbles to blow – or a bubble machine.
Auditory	• buckets – metal ones are good for the sound they make but plastic will do; • music CD; • sound effects of wind on CD; • CD player; • wind machine or powerful fan.
Kinaesthetic	• clothes of different texture hanging from the clothes line; • tin bath or other receptacle for holding the water to play in and wash in; • soap; • bubble mixture; • sponges and flannels; • towels; • fans or wind machine.
Olfactory/ gustatory	• scented soap; • washing powder.

How to put it together

1. Collect the materials you need from the above list – you may not need all of them – it will depend on what your purpose is.
2. Tie a loop at each end of the lines. Attach the washing line to two anchor points on opposite sides of the room. If you want to be able to raise and lower the line then use the cleat system at one end of each line (Structures 1, page 11).
3. Hang clothes on lines leaving spaces between them – to allow students to hang other clothes up.
4. Set up the laundry basket with clothes spilling out of it.
5. Fill buckets with water of differing temperatures.
6. Have bubble mixture to hand close to buckets.
7. Fill enough bags with pegs so that each pair or small group can have a bag.
8. Set up CD player and choose music to be played in the background.
9. Position wind machine or powerful fan.

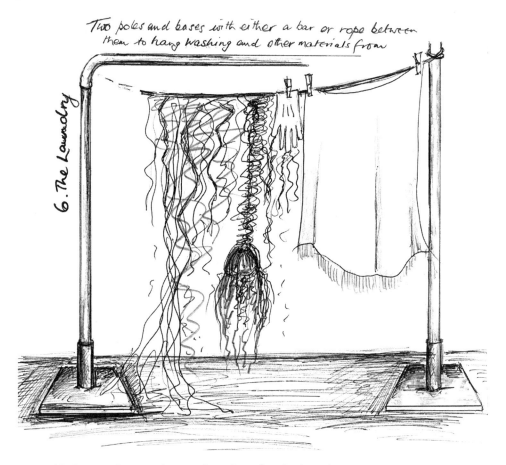

Figure 17 A way of suspending washing lines for the Laundry.

Ways to make use of the Laundry

Students help
to put up the
washing lines

A large pile of clothes in the centre of the room:

1. Small groups or individual students are given a task to collect a certain category of clothing from the pile such as: children's clothes, socks and tights, sports clothes, red ones, blue ones, etc.
2. When they have assembled their collection they peg them to a line.
3. The lines are then hung round the room to create the background for the sensory exploration or story etc. (below).

Sensory
exploration

The laundry as described has lots of opportunities for sensory exploration:

- students sorting out clothes into different colours, sizes, categories (trousers, tops, dresses, etc.);
- hanging up clothes on the lines;

- washing clothes in buckets of water and wringing them out;
- putting bare feet and hands into the buckets of water with and without bubble mixture;
- introducing a strong wind into the story and waving the washing lines over the group with accompanying sound effects;
- blowing bubbles.

Meet a character

As a setting for a character

This is a quick way to provide a setting to meet a character. By hanging appropriately coloured or textured fabric from the washing line as for storytelling below, you can create a simple setting for a character in role. For example a grubby and threadbare blanket could be the setting for a homeless person, silky blue material to meet Neptune or black and grey fabrics for a witch.

1. **The laundry woman** who works here appears (from behind the washing lines or even from within the laundry basket for a surprise entrance). She invites the students to help her because she has so much to do. She asks them if they will help her:
   - sort the clothes;
   - wash some of them in the buckets;
   - hang them on the line;
   - gather clothes together when the wind gets up and a storm threatens.

Listening – P Level 5 – Pupils to follow requests and instructions containing two key words

2. **A mother and son at home.** The washing line with clothes hanging out to dry gives a very simple and clear message of domesticity for a scene in a story about a mother and son at home. Nothing else is needed to convey the message that this was a scene 'at home'.

Blowing a gale

1. Put on wind machine and spin students in wheelchairs around in the wind.
2. Wave lines of washing in front of them to make physical contact with their faces and bodies as they pass.

Storytelling

1. Hang a piece of fabric from the line and sit in front of it to tell a story. This gives a clear and uncluttered background for the students to look at while being read to.
2. Choose a piece of fabric that relates to the story – shiny whites and blues for *The Snow Queen*, greens and browns to represent the forest for *The Three Bears* or a camouflage net for Michael Morpurgo's *War Horse*.

Numeracy
- finding pairs of socks;
- counting articles of washing in certain categories – trousers, tops, different colours, etc.

Maths Using and Applying – P Level 5 – Pupils sort or match objects

Art and craft   **To display students' work**
This is a convenient and quick way to display students' work. Simply peg the pictures onto the washing line and display the work of the students for everyone to see and appreciate.

Laundry in action

One example of how this environment has been used

Bamboozle uses the washing lines to create the setting for *Soap and Suds* – a PMLD performance that is designed to tour into schools. It therefore needs to be able to be put up and taken down quickly – which is much the same requirement for many environments that you might put up in schools.

For *Soap and Suds* we use five poles and bases (see Structures 3, page 12) set out in a pentagon shape with lines hung with clothes to enclose a space where the action takes place. We put weights (bags of sand covered in fabric) on the bases to increase the stability. Inside the space is a washing machine, some baskets of clothes, soap and water and a keyboard. The students come into the space in their wheelchairs brushing through or ducking under the washing as they enter.

The washing serves to enclose the space, masking any distractions on the walls of the hall and giving a sense of intimacy for the participants during the interactions of the performance.

Suggested learning outcomes

Listening – P Level 5 – Pupils to follow requests and instructions containing two key words

Maths Using and Applying – P Level 5 – Pupils sort or match objects

Part 2

Newsprint

Chapter 7

Snowfield

This environment is very suitable for involving the students in helping to set it up.

What is set up as your students enter the room

At the start   The sides of the room are hung with blue and white fabric; icicle-shaped lengths of shiny silver card are suspended from the ceiling.

A sheet of ice-blue fabric billows in the wind from a fan. Covering the floor is a snowfield – loosely screwed up newsprint half a metre deep in some places.

Bubble wrap is taped to the floor. Bowls of water – some with ice in – are placed round the floor.

Different sensory channels

Visual	• snow made from loosely screwed up newsprint; • white, blue and silver fabrics; • silver icicles.
Auditory	• sound of cold wind etc. from CD player; • sound of the wind caused by fan or wind machine.
Kinaesthetic	• loosely screwed newsprint heaped on the floor for the students to walk through. The students can walk barefoot; • bowls with water and ice; • feel of wind from wind machine/fans.
Olfactory/ gustatory	• scented herbs, or eucalyptus oil.

Equipment needed

How much equipment you need will depend on how complex you want to make the environment. If it is being put up for a short time you might decide just to use the snowfield. If it is going to be in situ for a couple of weeks or a whole term then it may well be worth the time and trouble to add in some of the other elements too.

The basic environment	• white, blue and silver fabric; • newsprint to be loosely screwed up and heaped on the floor; • newsprint torn up for blizzard.
Visual	• white tissue paper for snow fall; • bucket for torn up tissue paper for snow fall; • silver shiny card for icicles.
Auditory	• bubble wrap for the floor; • tape to stick down the bubble wrap; • CD player; • sound effects of wind blowing and ice cracking; • music.
Kinaesthetic	• a fan for chill effect; • hairdryer for snow fall; • wind machine for more forceful blizzard; • three bowls with warm, tepid and cold water in them; • ice for very cold water; • towels for drying after experiencing water.
For literacy idea/s	• paper with letters and words on them.

How to put it together

1. Collect the materials you need from the above list – you may not need all of them – it will depend on what your purpose is.
2. Suspend blue and white fabric from the walls. This could be done on all sides of the room for total effect or just along one side to provide a backdrop for the activities. Including some silver or shiny fabric among the blues and whites adds to the effect.
3. Make and suspend the icicles.
4. Tape down the bubble wrap onto the floor.
5. Screw up the newsprint. Keep it fairly loose to give plenty of volume. The students can be involved in doing this before you start – or as part of the process of setting up the environment.
6. Position the fan/s or wind machine.
7. Fill bowls with water (warm, tepid and cold) and one with ice and place in position.
8. Have paper with letters and words on to hand for literacy games.

Ways to make use of the Snowfield

Explore environment	• walk through the snow; • crunch over bubble wrap in chairs or with bare feet; • put hands into bowls of water of differing temperature, warm, cool, cold, with ice, etc.; • see also Chapter 9, Snowballs, page 77 for related activities.

P Level 2 (i)/(ii) – To accept and engage or cooperate with shared exploration

| Create snow fall/blizzard | 1. Gentle snow fall: tear up tissue paper into snowflake-sized pieces and scatter them above a hairdryer pointing towards the ceiling. The tissue is therefore blown into the air and when you turn the hairdryer off the pieces float down in a remarkably similar way to falling snow flakes. Lovely.
2. For a blizzard a more powerful wind source is needed such as a wind machine. We have found that almost all students love the feel of a wind in their faces. When you drop large handfuls of torn up newsprint in front of a wind machine the students get the experience of walking, or wheeling their chairs, into a simulated blizzard. |
|---|---|
| Make soundscapes | By handling newsprint students can make a whole variety of sounds from noisily screwing it up into balls to delicately tearing small pieces. Gather your students round the newsprint snowfield either in chairs or among the snow on the floor. Invite each one to invent a noise that the others then all copy. Continue round the circle. |
| Numeracy | Simple number games of collecting 2 or 3 or 10 or more snowflakes each. |

Maths Using and Applying – P Level 5 – Pupils make sets that have the same small numbers

| Literacy | 1. Write a letter on each of several pieces of newsprint and students put them together in order, e.g. c – a – t.
2. Write a word on each of several pieces of paper then students put them in order, e.g. the – cat – sat – on – the – mat. This could be supplemented with pictures or symbol cues. |
|---|---|

Writing – P Level 6 – Pupils copy letter forms

Writing – P Level 7 – Pupils group letters and leave spaces between them

Science	Put hands into bowls of water of differing temperature, for example warm, tepid and cold. See what the temperature of the water in the tepid bowl feels like after your hand has been in the warm one compared with how it feels after your hand has been in the cold bowl.

Snowfield in action

One example of how this environment has been used

This example is from a Bamboozle residency with families who have a child with PMLD, and included siblings. We used the story *We're Going on a Bear Hunt* by Michael Rosen, illustrated by Helen Oxenbury, as the stimulus that has a wealth of multi-sensory opportunities. The story takes us on a journey through a number of multi-sensory landscapes – swishy swashy grass, squelch squerch mud and so on until coming to the '. . . the swirling whirling snowstorm . . .'.

The environment we used for the snowstorm was very much as the one described in the 'What is set up as your students enter the room' section above (page 67).

We had a large amount of screwed up and torn up newsprint spread over the floor and a powerful wind machine.

To pass through the snowstorm each student took turns to be wheeled in their chair into the wind. The siblings had lots of fun throwing the paper into the wind so that the children in the chairs received a full sensory experience (!) of 'snow' and wind in their faces while being whirled around in their chairs.

Suggested learning outcomes

P Level 2 (i)/(ii) – To accept and engage or cooperate with shared exploration

Writing – P Level 6 – Pupils copy letter forms

Writing – P Level 7 – Pupils group letters and leave spaces between them

Maths Using and Applying – P Level 5 – Pupils make sets that have the same small numbers

Chapter 8

Projection Screen

Projecting images onto a screen has many uses. The question is what to use as a screen? A projector screen or interactive whiteboard will do the job, but look as if they belong in the corporate training room or conventional class lesson. Using newsprint to create a screen can give it a more creative feel and you can make it much bigger.

This is an environment that would be set up before students arrive.

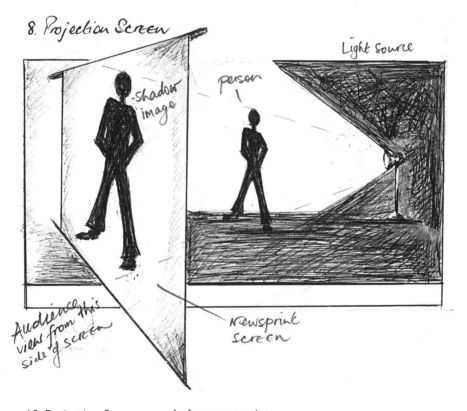

Figure 18 Projection Screen – made from newsprint.

What is set up as your students enter the room

At the start   Towards one side of the room is a big sheet of newsprint serving as a projection screen.

The screen will be used to project shadow puppets onto or for the silhouette of a character from a story.

The students gather in front of the screen on chairs or mats on the floor.

Different sensory channels

Visual
- images on the newsprint projection screen;
- a light source behind the screen;
- shapes of shadow puppets;
- colours of cellophane – part of the shadow puppets;
- silhouette shape of a character from a story or drama.

Auditory
- CD of music to accompany shadow play or introduction of character.

Kinaesthetic
- the tactile experience of making the shadow puppets;
- operating the puppets.

Equipment needed

How much equipment you need will depend on how complex you want to make the environment.

The basic
environment
- newsprint to make projection screen;
- means of suspending the screen:
  - clothes rail;
  - length of garden cane or timber;
  - tape for securing newsprint to the rail or cane and floor;
- means of projecting an image (OHP or AV projector) or giving a light for a shadow play (OHP, stage lantern).

Visual   Materials to make shadow puppets:
- card to cut out shapes;
- cellophane to add colour;
- sellotape;
- sticks to hold the puppet;
- scissors.

Auditory
- small percussion instruments;
- CD of sound effects;
- CD player.

Kinaesthetic
- mats and cushions to sit on.

For drama/
storytelling   Basic costume for character. One that will give a distinctive silhouette works well – a cloak, a wide brimmed hat, a spear or umbrella.

How to put it together

1. Collect the materials you need from the above list – you may not need all of them – it will depend on what your purpose is.

2. Making the screen can be done in a number of ways (the one you use will depend on how big you need it, whether it needs to be moveable, how long it can stay in situ, what other uses it needs to be put to as part of the activity you are doing):

    (a) **On a clothes rail** like the ones market traders use. This has the advantage of being easy to move about – especially if it is one that has wheels. It also has a rigid metal frame that makes it easy to tape the newsprint to and to stretch the paper tight thereby making a smooth screen.

    (b) **Suspended from a baton.** If you need a very large screen then fixing the newsprint to a baton near the ceiling and down on the floor is ideal. If you have fixtures (Structures 1, page 11) at ceiling level then attaching the paper to a garden cane or piece of dowelling and suspending the cane from the fixtures will do the job. The bottom of the screen can simply be taped down to the floor. Hanging things in high places is facilitated if you have in place the cleat system (see Structures 1, page 11) as this avoids the need for ladders.

    (c) **Screen as part of another structure.** You can use newsprint to build structures such as tunnels, dens or tepees. Make a structure out of garden canes tied or taped together to use as the framework and then cover with newsprint. The sides of the structure can then be used to project images onto the outside or you can put a light inside and use it as a shadow screen for a puppet show.

3. Place the light source behind the screen. An overhead projector, AV projector or floor-mounted stage light will do. Decide on the distance between light and screen. The further apart they are the more flexibility you have for size variation.

4. Collect materials for shadow puppet making.

5. Collect costume for character.

6. Collect CD player and music/sound effects if using.

Ways to make use of the Projection Screen

Meet a character

Having a character seen as a silhouette at first behind the screen and then bursting through creates a dramatic moment in any story or drama!

If your story or drama has a 'baddy' then he could at first appear as a silhouette behind the screen – with, for example, a wide brimmed hat and spear. This gives the silhouette clarity – it's not just a man. Students can go up to the screen and speak to him and have a conversation through the paper screen. Then at a dramatic moment he can burst through the screen to confront the group. This type of scenario is not for the faint hearted!

Another more restrained version is that the character comes up to the screen and carefully cuts a very small hole in it which he gradually makes bigger until he can see through it sufficiently to ask the students for help . . .

Listening – P Level 7 – To attend to and respond to, questions from adults about experiences, events and stories

Shadow puppetry

Make shadow puppets:
- cut out card shapes of people, animals, parts of landscape required for the story;
- to add colour cut holes in the card and cover the holes with cellophane. This is particularly successful with butterflies and similarly colourful creatures;
- attach sticks to the creatures so that they can be held up against the screen by the students who keep their own silhouette out of sight below the play board; the play board is the shadow of the ground at the bottom of the screen upon which the puppets can stand;
- make a mini-shadow screen out of a hoop or willow ring (see Figure 19 below);
- create a story for the shadow puppets to be part of;
- enact the story.

Art – P Level 5/P Level 6 – Pupils handle and use tools purposefully. Pupils show an intention to create

Figure 19 Mini-projection screen made from a circle willow.

Creating
soundscapes

Students can make up a soundscape to accompany the shadow play. This can be recorded and played while the story is acted out or can be played live by some students while others operate the puppets.

Projecting
landscapes

Having a large screen allows you to project a photograph or a video clip through a laptop and projector. For example a photo of the devastation of no man's land for a scene in the trenches of World War I (page 91), or a video clip of the ocean to give a wide backdrop for an island drama.

Science

1. Experiment with the distances between the light source, the screen and the object (shadow puppet or character). Discover the variations in focus and size as the object moves towards or away from the screen.
2. Students can experiment with scale by standing between the light source and screen to observe the difference their position makes to the size of image projected on the screen.

Science – P Level 7 – Pupils can demonstrate simple properties of light

Displaying
students'
work

Projecting students' work onto a screen is a great way to create an atmosphere and raise the status of the students by showing their work enlarged.

Projection Screen in action

One example of how this environment has been used

In a residency the students were on a quest to rescue a woman who was lost in the mountains. We wanted to heighten the tension by introducing a challenge in the form of a powerful and mysterious character.

We set up a newsprint screen behind which the character was first to appear in silhouette and projected a strong light onto the screen from behind him thus creating a shadow on the screen. He wore a hooded cloak and held a spear, making for a strong and simple visual image. We gave him a microphone to create a loud and booming voice. We also moved him a little way back from the screen towards the light source to make his shadow bigger than life-size on the screen.★

When all was ready the students gathered in front of the unlit screen but with some distance between them and it. We used narration to introduce the character: 'As the men and women rested in the mountains they saw in front of them the shadow of an enormous figure blocking the path . . .'

★ A balance has to be struck here between the increase in size you get moving the character away from the screen and nearer the light source and the decrease in focus you get as a result. Sometimes a fuzzy image is fine but if you want the image sharp and clear then the character has to stand close to the screen. There is the possibility of playing with scale by having two characters – one close by and therefore life-size and one further back and larger than life.

The light was then brought up to reveal the shadow of the man. The students were fearful initially and decided that they should first try to negotiate with the man and devised some questions to ask him. These were asked by the students making the journey up to the screen and speaking through it to the man and bringing the answers he gave back to the group waiting at a distance. We did not want to make it easy for the students to negotiate this obstacle so the man was unhelpful and obstructive at first. After some time he grew fed up with their demands and questions and became angry. He suddenly thrust his spear into the paper screen and leapt through it with a shout! This had considerable impact! With screams and nervous laughter on the part of the students and fear from the man to find so many of them. It transpired that the man was actually frightened and unhappy because no one seemed to like him and everyone who came along was afraid of him. This scenario provided an illustration of the notion that first appearances can deceive.

Suggested learning outcomes

Art – P Level 5/P Level 6 – Pupils handle and use tools purposefully. Pupils show an intention to create

Listening – P Level 7 – To attend to and respond to, questions from adults about experiences, events and stories

Science – P Level 7 – Pupils can demonstrate simple properties of light

Chapter 9

Snowballs

This is among the simplest and quickest of the environments to set up. The students can be presented with it as a ready-made environment but they may well also like being involved in making the snowballs.

What is set up as the students enter the room

At the start   From outside the closed door the sound of wind can be heard.

Inside, the floor is piled with heaps of snowballs made from loosely screwed up newsprint. Inverted umbrellas hang from the ceiling. There are buckets, baskets and other containers placed among the snowballs.

Different sensory channels

Visual
- a heap of snowballs, made by loosely screwing up newsprint;
- a fan blowing chilly wind on the students' faces;
- buckets, baskets and other containers for the students to throw the snowballs into;
- umbrellas hanging from ceiling.

Auditory
- sound of wind blowing;
- sound of cracking ice when bubble wrap is walked on or wheeled over;
- sound of screwing up and tearing paper.

Kinaesthetic
- newsprint paper snowballs;
- bubble wrap;
- chilly wind blowing;
- feel of the buckets, baskets and containers.

Equipment needed

This is a simple and quick environment to put together. If you decide to leave out the suspended camouflage net and umbrellas and get the students involved with making the snowballs then there is no preparation other than collecting the materials.

The basic environment	• rolls of newsprint for making snowballs; • blue camouflage net to suspend above the ceiling.
Visual	• umbrellas; • string to hang umbrellas from camouflage net; • buckets; • baskets; • containers; • tape for sticking bubble wrap down.
Auditory	• CD player; • sound effect CD of wind blowing; • bubble wrap on the floor.
Kinaesthetic	• fan.

How to put it together

1. Collect the materials you need from the above list – you may not need all of them – it will depend on what your purpose is.
2. Suspend camouflage net from ceiling by means of hooks (Structures 1, page 11).
3. Hang umbrellas from net.
4. Stick lengths of bubble wrap on the floor. If you stick bubble wrap on the floor under the snowballs then the students walking over them make the sound of cracking ice. This makes a great sound when wheelchairs run over the bubble wrap.
5. Make snowballs by loosely screwing up newsprint. This could be done by the students before, or as part of, your session.
6. Heap snowballs on top of the bubble wrap and on the floor.
7. Place buckets, baskets and containers among the snowballs.
8. Place fan in position.
9. Set up CD player and sound effects of the wind blowing.

Ways to make use of Snowballs

Explore environment	1. Walk across, or wheel across, the bubble wrap 'ice' and through the snowballs. 2. Pick up the snowballs and throw them into the suspended umbrellas or buckets and containers. 3. Have a snowball fight with teams behind lines throwing the balls at each other, or randomly across a circle sitting round the snowball pile. The great thing is that, unlike the real thing, these snowballs can be thrown as hard as you like and they will do no harm because they are so light. 4. Make a pile of snowballs and wade through them barefoot – if the pile of snowballs is deep enough then this also works for wheelchair users. 5. Throw them all up in the air together and watch them come down on top of the group.

| Make soundscapes | Newsprint can make a whole variety of sounds from noisily screwing it up into balls to delicately tearing small pieces. |

Make soundscapes

Newsprint can make a whole variety of sounds from noisily screwing it up into balls to delicately tearing small pieces.

1. Gather your students round a pile of snowballs either in chairs or among the snow on the floor. Invite each one to invent a noise that the others then all copy. Continue round the circle.
2. Students with more complex needs could be encouraged to turn towards or search for sounds as paper is scrunched, ripped etc.

P Level 1(i) – To show simple reflex responses

P Level 1(ii) – Pupils show emerging awareness of activities or experiences

P Level 3(ii) – Pupils use emerging conventional communication

Storytelling The setting could be used to tell the story of the Snow Queen, or of a historical polar exploration or ascent of Everest.

Listening – P Level 7 – Pupils listen, attend to and follow stories for short stretches of time

Numeracy
1. Simple counting. How many umbrellas are there? How many buckets/baskets and containers?
2. Everyone throws snowballs into the umbrellas or buckets and containers. Count how many balls are in each umbrella or container.
3. How many balls does it take to completely cover one of the students so that he (or she) can't be seen?

Maths Number – P Level 6 – Pupils join in rote counting to five. Count reliably to three

Snowballs in action

One example of how this environment has been used

This example happened by accident during some work with a group of students who were making up a story. The story involved the group going on a journey across a landscape that included, among other things, a snowfield made from screwed up newsprint and a series of inverted umbrellas hanging from the ceiling of the studio.

Towards the end of one day when the activities we had planned came to a natural conclusion, we were left with about 10 minutes until the session was due to end. To make use of this time we invited the students to explore again, in any way they liked, the environments through which they had recently journeyed. One student, Edward, made a beeline for the snowfield and spent the entire time screwing up the newsprint into snowballs and throwing them into one of the upturned umbrellas.

At the end of the week his parents reported that Edward, a student who did not readily communicate, had been very enthusiastic about this activity and explained to them many times what he had been doing.

This example provided a reminder for us that sometimes just putting a stimulus in front of students is all we need to do. Simply standing back and observing can be a very effective way of enabling students to become engaged in their own agenda.

Suggested learning outcomes

P Level 1(i) – To show simple reflex responses

P Level 1(ii) – Pupils show emerging awareness of activities or experiences

P Level 3(ii) – Pupils use emerging conventional communication

Maths Number – P Level 6 – Pupils join in rote counting to five. Count reliably to three

Listening – P Level 7 – Pupils listen, attend to and follow stories for short stretches of time

Chapter 10

Floor Covering

This environment works best when set up before the students arrive. Drawing on the paper is an activity that is accessible to all abilities and gives students who have PMLD a more level playing field with other students.

What is set up as your students enter the room

At the start   The students enter to find the floor covered with large sheets of newsprint – big enough to accommodate the whole group sitting on it. Students are invited to sit around the sheet with chairs and wheelchairs standing fully on the newsprint.

Each student is given a withy that is long enough to reach the floor from the sitting position and which has a marker pen taped to the end. They are then able to move their withy around and make marks on the paper sheet on the floor.

Baskets of fruit on tables at the side or on the floor.

Different sensory channels

Visual
- the large area of floor covered with newsprint;
- withies, or similar flexible length of rod, with a marker pen attached to one end of each;
- the students sit around on the newsprint using chairs and wheelchairs;
- they make marks and drawings on the newsprint with the help of marker pen attached to the withy.

Auditory
- music played in the background on a CD player or live.

Kinaesthetic
- the newsprint stuck on the floor with masking tape, the students feel the newsprint with their feet;
- withies which spring in the hand when drawing with them;
- the touch of the fruit – whole and squashed.

Olfactory/ gustatory
- taste of fruit;
- smell of fruit.

Equipment needed

How much of this you need will depend on the activities you will use it for.

The basic environment	• newsprint; • masking tape to stick it down; • plastic sheet beneath the newsprint. This is essential if you are using the fruit for painting as it will bleed through the paper as will some marker pens.
Visual	• withies – enough for each student to have two or three as one on its own with a marker pen attached may be too flimsy to allow much control; • marker pens; • tape to attach pens to withies.
Auditory	• CD player; • music on CDs.
Kinaesthetic	• chairs; • baskets for fruit.
Olfactory/gustatory	• fruit – different sorts; some soft fruit that can by squashed to produce puree; • bowls to put squashed fruit puree into; • knife for cutting up fruit; • plates to pass round the pieces of fruit on.

How to put it together

1. Collect the materials you need from the above list – you may not need all of them – it will depend on what your purpose is.
2. Lay out several lengths of newsprint next to each other on the floor and stick them together and to the floor with masking tape.
3. Fix a marker pen to one end of each withy – enough for every student to have at least one. It may be advantageous to tape two or three withies together as one on its own can be too flimsy for the student to be able to exert much control over it. Taping two together gives more control without it becoming rigid. You want to retain the flexibility of the withies as that accentuates the amount of movement that the student who has limited control of her movements can exert.
4. Collect the fruit and put in baskets.
5. Squash some soft fruit – e.g. raspberries – to make a juice for finger painting or drawing with.

Ways to make use of Floor Covering

Create a collective work of art	For this activity each student needs a withy with a felt pen taped to the end of it. The wheelchairs (or chairs) are placed in a circle round the edge of but completely on the sheet of newsprint so that there is paper all round

each chair. The advantage of using withies is that the length and flexibility of the stick accentuates the amount of movement the student gets by applying a small movement of their hand.

Each student then holds the withy in her hand and moves it to make lines on the paper on the floor. By using different colours and moving students to different positions on the paper they can achieve a Jackson Pollock-like work of art that can then be hung on the wall.

For students who find gripping a thin stick difficult it is helpful to make the stick larger by attaching a piece of pipe lagging or other such material to the end of it to make a fatter handle.

One advantage of this activity is that there is no right or wrong about what the students do. There is no judgement to be made. The marks they make are the marks they make. Not good, not bad, just accepted as their contribution.

P Level 2(ii) – Perform actions by trial and improvement

P Level 3(i) – To participate in shared activities with less support. Observe the results of their own actions with interest

Recording achievement
After they have created a work of art (above) you can then use the resulting multi-coloured sheet to record the achievements of each student. This could be done by writing their name beside the marks they have made on the floor and then under their name make a list of their achievements during the session; or indeed during the day or week if the sheet stays in place for longer than the one session.

Art and craft
Finger painting with squashed fruit.
This is a particularly kinaesthetic activity where the students can crush soft fruit into a bowl or bucket using their hands or beneath their feet and then use the resulting mixture of juice to draw patterns on the paper.

Hand and foot prints
Place the fruit in a bowl large enough to accommodate students' feet and hands. Students squash the fruit with hands and feet and then tread on the paper to make patterns.

The newsprint will need a plastic sheet under it for this activity as the fruit juice tends to bleed through the newsprint. An alternative would be to use thicker paper for this activity such as sugar paper or rolls of decorator's lining paper.

Art – P Level 4 – Pupils are aware of starting and stopping a process. They make marks intentionally on a surface with fingers or tools

Tasting and smelling	A fruit tasting session. Cut fruit into small pieces to release juice and smell and make them more manageable – and they will go further too!

Floor Covering in action

One example of how this environment has been used

We used a combination of the giant piece of artwork and record of achievement described above.

During a two-day residency for students who have complex needs and their parents we set up a very large sheet of newsprint paper on the floor. As many of the students had limited arm movement we placed the wheelchairs and chairs of the non-wheelchair users well onto the paper. The students, parents and artists then all had withies and drew patterns on the floor. We had music playing to accompany the activity – as well as providing an auditory experience music also takes the focus off the drawing thus reducing the possibility of feeling judged, which can happen when students are invited to draw. After some time we moved the chairs back and viewed the art work and wrote each of our names next to our creations.

At the end of each morning and afternoon session we gathered round the paper and one at a time wrote beside everyone's name what they had enjoyed about the morning's activities. At the end of the two days there was a record of what each person had engaged in and enjoyed. Our intention for doing this was to bring everyone together at the end of the session to recognise what we had done. It was not done to create a record of achievement as such but that is in effect what it was. We cut up the artwork and each of the families took their section home.

Suggested learning outcomes

P Level 2(ii) – Perform actions by trial and improvement

P Level 3(i) – To participate in shared activities with less support. Observe the results of their own actions with interest

Art – P Level 4 – Pupils are aware of starting and stopping a process. They make marks intentionally on a surface with fingers or tools

Chapter 11

Pile of Paper

This is one of the simplest environments to create and can be set up in a few minutes. The students can be involved in making the newsprint into balls by loosely screwing them up. However if you are planning a surprise as part of the activity (see below) it will be necessary to involve the students in screwing up the paper before a break and introducing the activity when they return to the room.

What is set up as your students enter the room

At the start   In the centre of the room a pile of loosely screwed up newsprint about a metre high and three metres across. A light shines on it. The rest of the room is in darkness.

The students are brought into the room quietly one by one and invited to sit on mats around the mound of paper.

Calming music plays.

Different sensory channels

Visual
- a heap of paper made of loosely screwed up newsprint;
- a spotlight directed on the mound or hung above it;
- any objects you choose to hide and use.

Auditory
- music;
- sound of handling paper – screwing it up, tearing it;
- sounds made by unseen person under paper.

Kinaesthetic
- paper can be felt by the students as they handle it and play with it;
- physically rolling in the paper;
- being completely covered by paper;
- the texture of the objects.

Equipment needed

How much of this you need will depend on the activities you will use it for.

The basic environment	• roll of newsprint.
Visual	• hanging light or angle poise; • objects for hiding.
Auditory	• CD player; • CD of calming music.
Kinaesthetic	• carpet squares or mats for sitting on.
Numeracy	• pieces of paper with a number (e.g. 1–10) on each.

How to put it together

1. Loosely screw the newsprint into balls and make a mound in the centre of the room.
2. The mound can be as high as you like – around a metre high and three metres across makes a good size for activities and is necessary if you are going to hide someone under it – see 'Meet a character' below. If you are not hiding a person then a much smaller mound will be sufficient for most of the activities.
3. Provide the hidden person with a means to make a noise – whistle, recorder etc.
4. Collect any objects you intend using.

Ways to make use of Pile of Paper

Explore environment	• sit round the pile of paper and observe it; • walk/crawl through it – move wheelchairs through it; • students (and staff!) love rolling about in it; • students take turns in being completely covered – we have done this with students while they remain in their wheelchairs; • have snowball fights – throwing snowballs across the pile at each other; • tear it up into small pieces and throw them up in the air to create snow fall; • get the group to wonder how else they can use it; • see also Chapter 7, Snowfield and Chapter 9, Snowballs for additional activities.
Meet a character	As the students come in there is someone concealed under the pile of paper. The students sit round the pile and you say, with a sense of intrigue, 'So here we have a pile of paper . . .' and pause. During the pause the concealed person makes a sound – a vocal sound or blows a whistle or knocks two stones together. They need to be able to make the sound without moving and disturbing the paper. My experience is that students don't notice the sound at first so it may need repeating several times, getting louder until the group are attentive. At a verbal cue from you such

as 'What do you think is making that noise?', the person leaps up scattering paper everywhere. This usually causes everyone to jump followed by peals of laughter.

You could then go on to an exploration of the paper as above or the character could have a message for them which leads into some drama – or she has a story to tell and the group gathers round to listen.

P level 2(i) – Pupils begin to show interest in people, events and objects

Puppetry and storytelling

Make fast puppets by screwing up the paper. This can be done as a story is read, for example, '*Once upon a time a little girl called Goldilocks . . .*'. Someone (or everyone) quickly screws up paper into a figure to represent Goldilocks. '*. . . and she went for a walk in the wood . . .*'; everyone screws up paper to make a tree. And so on through the story enacting it roughly as you go. The key is to do this fast and loose. Any old how will do – pass no comments on the quality of the representations, give no time for anyone to admire or comment on the models/puppets. It's a bit of fun – a lot of fun actually – and a great way of combating some students' perception that they are no good at art or making.

Make soundscapes

Make various sounds by
• tearing the paper in different ways and at differing speeds;
• screwing it up with different levels of vigour.
These can be recorded and played back as background to an activity.

Hide and seek

The pile of paper is a potential hiding place. You can place a number of objects beneath it for students to find.

Maths Shape, Space and Measure – P Level 6 – Pupils search for objects not found in their usual place

Numeracy

1. Concealed within the pile of paper are sheets of paper with numbers on. When they are discovered they are placed in order.
2. Putting paper pieces in order of size.
3. Gathering different shapes into piles – triangles, squares etc.

Maths Shape, Space and Measure – P Level 4 – Pupils search for objects that have gone out of sight

Pile of Paper in action

One example of how this environment has been used

We used the Pile of Paper activity during a Bamboozle residency to introduce a character to a story that the students were involved in making up. The character, Hern the Hunter, had been mentioned in the story but had not yet been encountered and we wanted to create a surprising and dramatic entry for him.

We put a pile of loosely screwed up newsprint about a metre high and several metres across in the centre of the studio. To one side of the studio hung a forest that had been made by the students earlier in the week – it was similar to the one described in Chapter 1, Musical Forest.

The setting was dimly lit with a spotlight on the pile of paper giving it importance and focus.

The group, who have varying degrees of learning ability, are told that they are to come in quietly and are brought into the space and sit on carpet squares placed in a circle round the pile of paper. Silence except for gentle guitar music in the background.

Then the sound of a pan pipe – not everyone hears it at first. It repeats, slightly louder, until everyone is aware that it is coming from beneath the paper. The paper stirs. The guitar becomes louder, more urgent. A girl claps with nervous tension. A pair of antlers appears out of the paper, followed by a masked figure – half deer, half person. The music builds – the students watch intently. The deer/human circles the pile of paper and disappears into the forest.

Suggested learning outcomes

P level 2(i) – Pupils begin to show interest in people, events and objects

Maths Shape, Space and Measure – P Level 4 – Pupils search for objects that have gone out of sight

Maths Shape, Space and Measure – P Level 6 – Pupils search for objects not found in their usual place

Part 3

Card and cardboard

Chapter 12

Trenches of World War 1

This environment is very suitable for involving the students in helping to set up the trench; this can help to get them to buy into the drama. It might, however, have greater immediate impact if it is set up before they arrive, thus preserving a 'wow' factor.

Figure 20 Lighting and a smoke machine create the atmosphere in no man's land. The trees are made from branches stuck into the plastic bases from garden sun shades. The lower part of the branch and the base is covered in modroc and painted. The floor has a sprinkling of bark chip (see Chapter 20, Woodland Floor), while fake barbed wire completes the picture.

What is set up as your students enter the room

At the start   As the students wait outside the room there is the sound of gunfire – a bombardment – heavy artillery and machine guns.

When they go through the door they are in a passage made from 2 metre high corrugated cardboard. The passage winds to and fro until they enter the room where there is a representation of a trench from World War I. It stands between half a metre and one metre above the floor; with sand bags, timber cladding and barbed wire. Beyond the trench a camouflage net hangs from the back wall with a space representing no man's land between the net and the trench. Wisps of smoke and low lighting add to the atmosphere.

The students gather in front of the trench . . .

Different sensory channels

Visual
- lighting effects – the flash of explosions;
- smoke machine if available;
- the angular shapes of the trench timbers and barbed wire;
- props – as below in 'Equipment needed' section.

Auditory
- sound effects of gunfire;
- sound effects of explosions;
- voice of soldier reading out his letter home as he writes it.

Kinaesthetic
- the ridged texture of the corrugated card;
- texture of the hessian sand bags;
- sand (if you decide to get students to fill the hessian bags themselves as part of the activity);
- barbed wire (imitation of course!); this is made of plastic so the sharp points are not entirely benign;
- handling props such as rifles, tin helmets etc.;
- emotional content of soldiers' letters to and from home;
- physical movement during the 'dying' workshop.

Equipment needed

How much equipment you need will depend on how complex you want to make the environment. If it is being put up for a short time you might decide just to put up the corrugated card trench and use barbed wire over chairs to represent the front line trench. If it is going to be in situ for a couple of weeks or a whole term then it may well be worth the time and trouble to add in some of the other elements too.

Basic
environment
- roll of corrugated card;
- camouflage net;
- hessian sacks;

- sand for sandbags (it is possible to substitute other materials to fill the bags, such as screwed up newspaper. However, sand gives the most authentic look and feel);
- timber lengths for the cladding of the trenches – slats from garden fencing are ideal;
- fake barbed wire.

Visual
1. Lighting for flashing of explosions – if no specialist lighting available then turning classroom lights on and off will create the effect;
2. Props – how far you go with these will depend on the purpose and length of the piece of work. Any or all of the following will add authenticity:
   - rifles;
   - metal mugs or eating utensils;
   - ammunition boxes;
   - boxes for soldiers to sit on;
   - paper for letter home;
   - something to write with – a pencil is more timeless and therefore more authentic than a biro;
   - photo of loved one – a sepia period photo would work well;
   - tin helmet for person playing the role of soldier.

Auditory
- pre-recordings of sound effects – bombardment, machine gun fire.

Kinaesthetic   Many of the props above (in Visual section) have differing textures and therefore kinaesthetic potential if opportunities for students to handle them are created.

How to put it together

1. Collect the materials you need from the above list – you may not need all of them – it will depend on what your purpose is.
2. Put up the corrugated card passageway to represent the trench leading to the front line trench.
3. Suspend the camouflage net from hooks in the wall or from the ceiling (Structures 1, page 11).
   If you are constructing the trench before the students enter – go to 4.
   OR: if you are going to get the students to build the trench themselves – go to 9.
4. Fill hessian sacks with sand – a few give the impression of a trench – the more you have the better the effect.
5. Fix the lengths of timber together – nailed onto a cross piece of timber.
6. Prop timber upright against the sandbags – leave a gap through which a soldier can climb into no-man's land.
7. Wind barbed wire around the timber and along the top of the barricade.
8. Place any props – rifles, stores, ammunition boxes, letters home, mugs for tea, tin helmets.
9. Lay out all the materials on the floor of the room when the students enter and invite them to configure the trench.

Ways to make use of Trenches of World War I

Students
build the
trench

Provide your students with empty hessian sacks, sand, lengths of timber such as garden fencing slats, fake barbed wire, string and weights of some sort and give them the task of creating a trench.

If authenticity of the trench is important you can give them a photograph of an actual trench so they can model what they build on it. Alternatively if you are simply looking for a trench to provide a vehicle to work with, for example, the letter home idea (below) you can give them the materials and accept whatever they put together as a representation of the trench.

Literacy

Collective writing. A letter home from the front

See a short piece of drama – a member of staff in role as a soldier in the trench – there is a lull in the bombardment and he is composing a letter home. Stop the action and with the whole group write the letter home that the soldier is composing. Use a large sheet of paper and gather the group where they can all see it then ask, 'If we were to make up the contents of the letter the soldier was writing home to his loved one/s who would he be writing to?', take suggestions and write them on the sheet before agreeing to whom this letter is to be addressed.

Then gradually construct an agreed letter.

Other questions that can help the process include:

'What name shall we give his wife/mother/sister/sweetheart?'

'What would he put first do we think?'

'Will he describe what it is actually like in the trench or will he make it sound better than it is, in an attempt to prevent his loved one from worrying?'

'Will he write about the trenches or ask about home; or both?'

'What might the censor allow to be said in a letter?'

When the letter is finished have the person who is representing the soldier go back into the trench and write the agreed words out while sheltering in the trench and voicing what he is writing as he does so. There could be a low-level sound effect of gun fire in the background as he writes.

Follow up activities could include the recipient receiving the letter – or the soldier receiving the reply.

Writing – P Level 7 – Pupils group letters and leave spaces between them as though they are writing separate words

Speaking – P Level 8 – Pupils take part in role play with confidence

Numeracy

Probability, fractions and percentages

The likelihood of a soldier surviving long in the trenches was slim. Around 75 per cent were killed according to one statistic. This gives an opportunity for some maths in the form of a probability exercise or one on percentages or fractions.

Figure 21 The trench seen here was made by students during a residency. They were given sawn lengths of timber, a couple of branches, sandbags and barbed wire to work with. This scene of a soldier with a letter followed the trench building. It is described in the Literacy activity above (page **94**).

The students become soldiers in the trenches before enacting 'going over the top'. They are each secretly given a slip of paper – three out of four slips have 'killed' on them, while one out of every four has 'lived' on it. The students look at their slip and keep it secret. At the order 'Advance' they clamber over the barricade in slow motion (easier to keep control). As they advance machine gun fire is heard. The ones with 'killed' on their slip enact a slow-motion death while the others manage to make it back to the trench.

Movement   Before this going over the top exercise you could do a movement session around slow-motion dying. This is generally very popular and is a good opportunity for controlled movement. The students are then prepared in advance for the death enactment to come.

Trenches of World War I in action

One example of how this environment has been used

This example is from a collaboration project between The National Theatre, three London special schools and Bamboozle. The week-long residency was based on the NT's production of *War Horse*, a story about a horse requisitioned by the army from a Devon farm to serve as a cavalry horse in France at the start of World War I.

During the early part of the week the students had built a trench – as described in the first section of 'Ways to make use of Trenches of World War I' (page 94). We set up the corrugated card so that when the students went through the door into the hall they entered the supply trench. Two lengths of corrugated card wound this way and that for about 25 metres to represent a supply trench leading to the front line. This meant that the students were unable to see what they were coming into until they had made the journey along the trench.

This project included a number of students who might be described as having challenging behaviour. On the fourth morning the students were lively for some reason and we felt that we needed to re-focus them on the work. To do this we decided to get them to enter the hall one at a time, which I find a very effective way of regaining focus and control. So we gathered them outside the hall door and told them that they were to be soldiers given the task of taking supplies to the front line. In a pile beside the door were boxes of stores, rifles, ammunition cases and other materials of war.

From inside came the sound of a bombardment and electric guitar music and, as the door opened to allow each student in, those waiting their turn caught sight of flashes of light from the explosions. It was clear that a dynamic experience was waiting beyond the doors!

Then, one at a time, they were invited to select an item from the pile of stores and proceed through the door into the trench. This slowed down their entry, giving us complete control over how they entered as well as building the suspense and sense of expectation.

This activity was pretty full on with a lot of noise, darkness and flashing lights. It would not be suitable for all groups. This group had been exploring the issues around the story of the horse and the trenches for three days before the activity described here, so they had been warmed up. Even so some students found going through the door a bit intimidating while others relished it. For those who needed more support we gave them time, reduced the volume and intensity, put some more lights on and sent a friend or member of staff with them to enable them to experience it.

Suggested learning outcomes

Writing – P Level 7 – Pupils group letters and leave spaces between them as though they are writing separate words

Speaking – P Level 8 – Pupils take part in role play with confidence

Chapter 13

Snow Queen's Castle

This can either be set up for the students to come into, or they can be involved in building the Snow Queen's Castle out of cardboard boxes beforehand.

What is set up as your students enter the room

At the start   The students wait outside the locked door. A howling wind can be heard punctuated with the sound of cracking ice. You unlock the door and open it slowly, cautiously.

Inside, opposite the door, steps lead to a raised platform on top of which stands the Snow Queen, dressed in white and blue. On either side of the steps are structures (made from cardboard boxes) covered with blue, white and shiny fabric representing her castle. To one side is the mouth of a cave suggesting a prison cell.

The floor is covered with snow – crumpled newsprint. Wind blows in the face of the Snow Queen moving hair and clothing.

The lighting is low with a focus on the Snow Queen and parts of the ramparts.

The students enter and sit on mats or chairs facing the castle.

Different sensory channels

Visual
- the floor covered with white crumpled newsprint;
- steps up to a platform where the Snow Queen stands;
- two cardboard structures on either side of the steps;
- a prison cave to one side of the Snow Queen's platform;
- fabric – whites, blues and silver – some shiny.

Auditory
- recorded sounds of howling and whistling winds;
- other sound effects – cracking of ice, howling wolves;
- wind from wind machine or fan;
- sound of newsprint 'snow' as it is walked through;
- soundscape created by students using percussion and paper.

Kinaesthetic	•	wind blowing on the face of the Snow Queen and students;
	•	feel of the crumpled newsprint over the floor.
Olfactory/ gustatory	•	exotic smells of herbs and perfumes, sandalwood and mint.

Equipment needed

How much equipment you need will depend upon how complex and detailed you want to make it and whether it will be in situ for a short or long period of time.

The basic environment	•	platform and steps to elevate the place where the Snow Queen stands – this is not essential but elevating the Queen adds to the sense of remoteness and power. A small stage block would also do the job;
	•	cardboard boxes of different sizes to form structures either side of where the Snow Queen stands;
	•	dispenser with parcel tape to fix the boxes together.
Visual	•	fabric – white and blue and some iridescent or sparkly to represent the shine of ice;
	•	newsprint screwed up loosely to represent snow;
	•	lights to focus on prominent places;
	•	different coloured paper, foil and cellophane to denote snow and ice.
Auditory	•	CD player to play sound effects;
	•	sound recordings of wind, cracking ice and the howling of wolves;
	•	percussion instruments for making soundscape;
	•	microphone and means to record the soundscape.
Kinaesthetic	•	fan or wind machine to blow wind on the face and hair of Snow Queen.
Olfactory/ gustatory	•	herbs – mint, sage;
	•	perfumes – sandalwood joss sticks.
For drama idea/s	•	costume for Snow Queen;
	•	costume for guard or the prisoner, Kay, if using. (For more about Kay see 'Meet and question the Snow Queen' below.)

How to put it together

1. Place the platform for the Snow Queen in position in the centre of the space facing the door through which the students will enter. Put steps or blocks in position to enable her to climb easily up and down.
2. Fix cardboard boxes together (see note below on fixing boxes together) using parcel tape to make two mounds on either side of the platform. If you have sufficient height then you can create an arch by putting canes across from the top of one mound to the other and building more boxes on top of the canes to complete the arch.
3. Configure the boxes on one side into the shape of a cave – large enough for at least one person to get into. Hang ragged fabric, or other materials, at the entrance to represent bars of Kay's prison.

4. Cover the boxes with white, blue and silver shiny fabric to represent ice and snow.
5. Loosely screw up newsprint to cover the floor in front of the castle to represent a snowfield.
6. Costume the Snow Queen. A full costume of whites, silver and blue with make-up to match would create impact but is not essential. Something – a cloak or scarf and crown will be sufficient to denote the role.
7. Arrange any lighting.
8. Set up CD player.
9. Put herbs in place and light sandalwood joss sticks if using.

Note on fixing boxes together. First you need to collect lots of cardboard boxes of varying sizes – the wider the range of sizes the more flexibility you will have to build with. An ideal range would be from a crisp box size to the size of box that a fridge freezer comes in, but any collection will do. Boxes that removal firms use are ideal as they are strong and can be used over and over again. Storage is relatively easy as they can be packed flat after use.

Then you open each box and put it into shape and tape it together – we use parcel tape on a dispenser as this is quickest and the tape can be easily split with a Stanley knife to pack them flat after use. Once you have your collection of boxes you can begin to build whatever it is you, or the students, want.

If you are building a particularly large structure – such as the Snow Queen's Castle here or Chapter 14, Sea Cave – with a lot of boxes piled up you may want to consider strengthening it. Ways to do this include:

*   taping each box onto the ones next to it, to prevent them slipping if knocked into;
*   putting a length or cane from top to bottom and taping it in place – this gives the whole structure more rigidity;
*   putting a weight in the boxes on the floor to make them more stable.

For any structure requiring an arch such as Chapter 14, Sea Cave (page 103), first build two piles of boxes the same height as each other and secure them. Then put a large box across the top of the piles. If the gap is too wide for the available boxes then lay two canes (or similar) from the top of one pile to the other, and build on top of the canes with more boxes.

The boxes are then covered with lengths of material to conceal the cardboard and give the 'look' that is required.

Ways to make use of Snow Queen's Castle

Students build environment	This environment is well suited to student involvement in making it. Tasks include: • putting together flattened cardboard boxes with parcel tape; • creating the structures of the castle by fixing the boxes together in two piles; • making decisions about the colours of fabrics and how to cover the structures to represent the Snow Queen's Castle; • screwing up newsprint for the snow.

Explore environment	Students can: • walk through the snow; • climb the steps to the Snow Queen's platform to see what difference it makes to be high up – typically being higher creates a feeling of power; • crawl into the cave prison to experience that feeling.
Make soundscapes	Students can create a soundscape to represent the landscape of ice and snow using: • percussion instruments; • their voices (blowing wind and howling wolves); • the newsprint – tearing slowly or screwing it up energetically etc. This could be devised, rehearsed and recorded and then the recording played back when the Snow Queen appears.
Storytelling	The environment could be used as a backdrop to tell the story of the Snow Queen or other stories set in such a landscape.

Meet and question the Snow Queen	This is an exploration of one moment in the story of the Snow Queen. The Snow Queen can be in position when the students enter the room as described in the first section above. This gives a dramatic start to the session.
	    The students are told that the Snow Queen that they see in front of them has captured a little boy, Kay, and has imprisoned him in her castle. If you have someone to represent Kay then you can enact this scene for the students to watch. Alternatively as the information is narrated the story-teller takes a jacket (to represent Kay) and places it in the cave.
	    The students are then asked to consider what questions they might ask the Queen in order to:
	• establish her motives;
	• see if they can negotiate a return of Kay;
	• find out the security features of the castle;
	• see if they might be able to rescue Kay.
	    The questions you invite them to come up with can be tailored to serve your learning outcomes and any individual targets students may have.
	    The students then ask the Queen the questions they have made up. The impact and significance of this process can be enhanced by staging it in a dramatic manner. Having a distance between the group and the Snow Queen's position means that the student/s has a journey to make before addressing the queen.
	    The answers they get to their questions can then be discussed in the group to decide how to proceed.

Speaking – P Level 6 – Pupils ask simple questions to obtain information

Numeracy   • counting the number of cardboard boxes;
            • sorting boxes into sizes to put the larger ones at the bottom when
              constructing the castle.

Maths Shape, Space and Measure – P Level 5 – To find big and small objects on request. To compare the overall size of one object with that of another

Art and craft   This activity provides an alternative to covering the structure of boxes with fabric to create the castle.

Each student or group of students has a box to decorate. They can choose from a range of materials – paper, pieces of fabric, paint – to create a box that is in keeping with the snow and ice of the environment. Keeping in the colour palette of white, blue and silver gives coherence to the result.

Art – P Level 7 – Working in two or three dimensions pupils intentionally represent an object. They purposefully choose colours or techniques

The boxes are then assembled to create the castle.

Science   Students work out the balance of the boxes on top of each other and how to construct the arch.

Snow Queen's Castle in action

One example of how this environment has been used

Bamboozle used this activity (more or less as described in the 'Meet and question the Snow Queen' section above) as the starting point for a week-long residency with 20 SLD/MLD students based on the story.

Students came into the space and settled down on carpet squares in front of the castle. When they were assembled I told them that they were going to see a short piece of action from a story about a Snow Queen and that all we had to do was to watch and listen.

The Snow Queen then entered bringing a small boy with her. She shoved him roughly into the prison, told him he will never escape and climbed the steps to look out across the castle battlements. We then stopped the action and asked the two people playing the Snow Queen and the boy to take off their costume and come and sit with the group (this was done so that there was no distraction while we discussed what had happened).

I then said to the students: **'What do we think might have been going on there? What did anyone notice?'** and took a piece of sugar paper to write down their suggestions verbatim. The students gave some observations and opinions about the Snow Queen's treatment of the boy. I divided the offerings into what we know and what we are guessing. For example, we know that she dragged the boy in holding his jacket; we are guessing that she is unkind. We know that she climbed the steps; we are guessing that the boy is alone.

After we had collected a lot of suggestions I said: **'If we were to ask the Snow Queen some questions to find out more, what might we ask?'** I find this a very useful structure to enable students to come up with ideas. Putting 'If we were to . . .' at the beginning is designed to make it non-threatening. 'If we were to – we're not necessarily going to, so we don't have to worry unduly about getting it right – I was just wondering . . .' Also saying **'What might we ask?'** has a similar function. I'm not saying that we are going to but just wondering, for argument's sake, what might we say if we did ask?

The students worked in groups and came up with questions about why the Snow Queen had put the boy in prison. They were then invited to go up to the Snow Queen to ask their questions. We wanted to make the process of asking the questions a significant challenge and to have a sense of occasion about it. We therefore got the Snow Queen back in costume and put her in place at the top of her steps. This gave her the sense of power that height provides.

When it was their turn to ask a question each student or students (some went up in pairs if they needed more support) made the journey from where they sat through the snow (newsprint screwed up on the floor) to the bottom of the steps and then addressed their question to the Snow Queen.

Before they left on their journey to the castle we discussed how to approach the Queen – would it be appropriate just to go up and ask their question? Should they wait for her to address them? How do they address a queen? This led to some fruitful discussion about appropriate behaviour and respect and delayed the moment of meeting the Queen thereby increasing the significance.

Suggested learning outcomes

Maths Shape, Space and Measure – P Level 5 – To find big and small objects on request. To compare the overall size of one object with that of another

Speaking – P Level 6 – Pupils ask simple questions to obtain information

Art – P Level 7 – Working in two or three dimensions pupils intentionally represent an object. They purposefully choose colours or techniques

Chapter 14

Sea Cave

This environment is most suited to be set up before the students arrive. However it is very possible to involve the students in adding elements to the cave.

What is set up as your students enter the room

At the start   Waiting outside the room the sound of the sea breathing on the shore and the cries of gulls can be heard.

The students enter to find a cave made from a pile of cardboard boxes of different sizes. The boxes are swathed in fabric – blues and greens, some plain, some iridescent – giving an impression of the sea. A net hangs over the mouth of the cave.

In front of the cave entrance an upturned wooden box – possibly used as a seat. There are shells and pebbles, a sprinkling of sand and other flotsam and jetsam washed up on the beach.

In front of the cave carpet squares indicate places to sit. The students gather.

The sound of the sea and the gulls fades . . .

Alternatively the students contribute to the cave environment

This is a way to increase student involvement in the drama or the activity. Before the students go into the room they are given an object – a shell or pebble or piece of flotsam, bit of rope, water worn wood etc. They are invited to go into the space, find the cave and place their object somewhere near the cave.

It is important that the students are allowed to put their object anywhere on or around the cave. In this way the students are brought into the drama because they are directly involved in helping to determine the look of the cave and its surroundings. The trick is that wherever they decide to place their objects is acceptable to us. When using this idea we need to remove from our own mind any concept of how it is supposed to look. Being disciplined about this will be well rewarded. If you need, for some reason, a piece of rope to be in a certain position around the cave then put it there yourself and give the students other objects that can go anywhere.

Different sensory channels

Visual	• shape of the cave; • different colours of the sea cave – greens and blues; • iridescent fabric twinkling in the light representing the surface of water; • shapes of shells, pebbles and flotsam and jetsam (plastic bottles, bits of string and rope).
Auditory	• sound of the sea (recorded); • cries of gulls (recorded); • sound of sea in a conch shell; • percussion soundscape made by students; • vocal soundscape made by students; • voice of character if used.
Kinaesthetic	• textures of sand, pebbles, shells, flotsam and jetsam.
Olfactory/ gustatory	• seaweed if available.

Equipment needed

How much equipment you need will depend on how complex you want to make the environment. If it is to remain set up for some time then the whole environment as described is worth putting in place. However if you want to just use the interaction with the character on the beach then place the seat and character in position and surround her with nets, shells and pebbles etc. to denote the seashore.

The basic environment	• a selection of cardboard boxes of varying sizes; • tape for taping them into position; • a pole and base (this is an optional extra – it would give the possibility of a flag flying from it or fishing nets hanging in the sun).
Visual	• a selection of blue and green fabric; • some iridescent or sparkly fabric to reflect light; • a flag – if using flag pole. This can be an old shirt, piece of material, or skull and cross bones.
Auditory	• CD player; • sound effects – recordings of sea and gulls; • conch shell – for listening to the sea; • percussion instruments for generating a sea soundscape.
Kinaesthetic	• netting to represent fishing nets; • sand; • pebbles; • shells; • flotsam and jetsam (plastic bottles, bits of string and rope).
Olfactory/ gustatory	• seaweed if recently collected.

For drama
idea/s

- wooden box or small stool for character to sit on;
- costume for the character inhabiting the cave. This can be a full costume but equally one item to represent the character will suffice. For example, a threadbare jacket for a castaway, a trident for Neptune, a bandanna for a pirate.

For literacy

- Bottle with message inside.

How to put it together

For a note on building with cardboard boxes see Chapter 13, Snow Queen's Castle – How to put it together section (pages 98–99).

1. Collect the materials you need from the above list – you may not need all of them – it will depend on what your purpose is.
2. Put the pole in its base (if using).
3. Tape the cardboard boxes together.
4. Arrange the boxes into two piles either side of what will become the cave entrance – make the entrance large enough to accommodate the character. Alternatively make the cave entrance just large enough for the character to crawl through from a larger space behind it.
5. Put a flat box across to join the tops of each of the two piles – this makes the roof of the cave.
6. Cover the boxes with blue, green and iridescent fabric.
7. Arrange the sand, pebbles, shells and seaweed, flotsam and jetsam on the ground in front of and around the cave.
8. Put the flag up the pole.
9. Place box in position in front of cave.

Ways to make use of the Sea Cave

Explore
environment

- students explore and handle the rich variety of textures in this environment;
- pass the objects round among students;
- students usually love to explore inside a cave.

P Level 1(ii) – Pupils have periods where they appear alert and ready to focus their attention on objects or parts of objects

Make
soundscapes

1. Students can experiment with percussion instruments to make the sounds of the sea. They can then play the soundscape as the character (below) walks along the beach.
2. Alternatively their soundscape can be recorded and played as background when the character appears. This has the advantage of enabling the students to focus on interacting with the character rather than concentrating on playing their instrument.

Music – P Level 8 – Pupils create their own simple compositions carefully selecting sounds

Meet a
character

A woman is sitting on the box whittling a stick as the students enter the room. When they are settled she stands up, looks along the beach and out to sea – as if searching for something. She sits down again.

The teacher asks a question such as:

- 'I wonder what is going on there.'
- 'What did anyone notice – what did we see or hear?'
- 'How do we think she might be feeling?'

These are non-judgemental questions that do not require a particular answer. This approach is designed to enable students to respond without fear of being wrong. You can write down what the students say on a large piece of paper as a way of giving value to their thoughts. The idea here is not for the students to guess the scenario but rather for you to give them the opportunity to say what they have noticed and come up with ideas about what might be going on.

This exercise can be followed up with speaking to the woman. 'Let's ask her to tell us something about how she came to be on the beach.' The character then reveals how she came to be there – her explanation might take on some of their wonderings – she was shipwrecked and needs help to build a boat to get her home.

Can the students help her make a boat?

Use the carpet squares to make into the shape of a boat.

Dismantle the cave and make the boxes into a boat.

Use any other solutions the students can come up with.

The woman gets in – uses the pole as a mast and sails away.

Listening – P Level 7 – Pupils attend to and respond to questions from adults and peers about experiences and stories

Numeracy

- simple counting: how many shells, pebbles, plastic bottles etc. are on the beach;
- comparisons – are there more pebbles than shells on the beach?
- put the pebbles in size or weight order; put the shells or pebbles into a spiral shape.

Maths Number – P Level 4 – Pupils show an awareness of number activities and counting

Literacy   **Make up a story**
You can wonder with the students whether anyone lives or lived in the
cave – if so who? What might they use it for? Where might they have come
from? How long did they stay there? Where did they go to? The students'
ideas could be made into a story that you write down.

Message in a bottle
The character finds a bottle washed up on the beach. There is a message in
it. The message is written in language that extends the vocabulary or levels
of understanding of your group. For example a message saying simply
'Help' raises some questions including: Who wrote the message? Who
needs help? How might we be able to help them?

Questions
Students work in small groups to come up with a question they would like
to ask the woman to find out more about her predicament. The questions
are then asked of the woman sitting on her box in front of the cave.

**Listening – P Level 8 – Pupils respond appropriately to questions about why
or how**

Figure 22 Here a rope laid out on the floor and surrounded by blue material gives the
shape of a boat and defines the space where the action will take place. The
white sheets are flown from the studio roof to give a suggestion of billowing
sail canvas. This is often an easier solution than trying to be too literal. Two
poles and bases (Structures 3, page 12) represent the masts and a pile of
baskets the cargo. This idea could be used to define the boat shape to help
the castaway escape from the island in 'Meet a character' (page 106).

Sea Cave in action

One example of how this environment has been used

This cave provided the starting point for a week-long residency.

The students entered the hall to the sound of the sea and gulls to find a cave – as described above in the 'What is set up as your students enter the room' section (page 103), but with pieces of driftwood added to give the impression that the woman may have built part of the cave as a shelter rather than it appear as a completely natural cave. There was a rope laid out to represent a shoreline, with sand, shells, pebbles, seaweed and flotsam scattered along it. Sitting in the entrance to the cave with her back to the shore was a woman in a threadbare jacket, torn-off calf-length trousers and bare feet.

When the students had settled on the carpet squares that were arranged along the shoreline, the music changed – live guitar was added above the recorded sound of waves on shore. The woman stood up, stretched, came to the shore and looked out to sea over the heads of the students. She took her time, she seemed to be looking for something; after a while she found nothing and returned to sit by her cave. She took a box from where it was hidden, opened it carefully, examined what was inside before replacing it in its hiding place and walking off along the beach.

The students were then invited to respond to what they had seen in the manner described in the 'Meet a character' section of 'Ways to make use of the Sea Cave' above (page 106).

They were asked: 'What did any of us notice there?' Their responses and wonderings led us to make up a story about a shipwreck, pirates and treasure.

Suggested learning outcomes

Level 1(ii) – Pupils have periods where they appear alert and ready to focus their attention on objects or parts of objects

Music – P Level 8 – Pupils create their own simple compositions by carefully selecting sounds

Listening – P7 – Pupils attend to and respond to questions from adults and peers about experiences and stories

Maths Number – P Level 4 – Pupils show an awareness of number activities and counting

Listening – P Level 8 – Pupils respond appropriately to questions about why or how

Chapter 15

Home on the Street

This environment is most suitable for setting up before the students arrive.

What the students see as they enter the room

At the start A woman is sitting hunched on the pavement of a road.

A polythene sheet is stretched above her, tent like, to give her some protection from the elements. She is clutching a blanket round her shoulders. She sits on flattened cardboard boxes with a threadbare sleeping bag over her knees. Next to her a bag, a polystyrene cup, a length of rope and a plastic bowl with water in it.

The sounds of melancholy music, babble of people on the street and cars speeding by, an occasional horn.

Different sensory channels

Visual
- the woman and her body language;
- a selection of items beside her – the cardboard boxes, sleeping bag, a bag, a cup, a plastic bowl of water etc.

Auditory
- the sound of the melancholy music – recorded or live if you have a musician;
- woman rummaging in her bag;
- woman sneezing, coughing;
- recorded sounds of the street, people talking, cars.

Kinaesthetic
- students exploring the items in the setting before the woman is in position;
- feelings prompted by her situation.

Olfactory/ gustatory
- woman can have food and/or drink (e.g. coffee) to smell or taste;
- students could give food to her.

Equipment needed

How much equipment you need will depend on how complex you want to make the environment. It can be set up as described above. An alternative is to have no setting, no sound effects, just a person wrapped in a blanket and carrying a bag.

The basic environment	• flattened cardboard boxes; • a polythene sheet.
Visual	• a shoddy blanket as costume – round woman's shoulders; • a threadbare sleeping bag; • a bag; • a cup; • length of rope; • a plastic bowl of water.
Auditory	• CD player; • CD of music; • sound effects CD of street sounds.
Kinaesthetic	• carpet squares or mats for students to sit on.
Olfactory/ gustatory	• food; • drink, e.g. coffee; • apple for woman.

How to put it together

1. Collect the materials you need from the above list – you may not need all of them – it will depend on what your purpose is.
2. Lay out some flattened cardboard boxes for the woman to sit on.
3. Stretch a rope like a clothes line between two points above the boxes.
4. Attach a piece of polythene to the line to make a shelter.
5. Assemble possessions and put them in position.
6. Set up CD player for music and sound effects.

Ways to make use of Home on the Street

Explore the home on the street	• observe the surroundings and the woman's belongings; • listen to the sounds of the street and the background melancholy music; • examine the tent of polythene, the texture of the blanket, sleeping bag etc.; • wonder about any of the items.
As a setting to meet a character	**Either:** The woman is already sitting as described above. **Or:** She can enter with blanket round shoulders and a bag, look round anxiously and then settle herself onto the boxes under the plastic sheet. Whichever scenario you choose the woman needs to do very little. Just enter, settle down, possibly take a bite out of an apple and then doze off.

The less the person playing the role does the better – the students can then come up with possible scenarios.

The students watch the action for about a minute, then the teacher/facilitator stops the action. Ask the person playing the role to come out of role and leave the blanket in the shelter and join the group. Removing the role means that there is not then a distraction when you do the next bit, which is:

The facilitator asks the students – 'So what did we notice?' or 'What do we think was going on there?' Make a list of contributions on a large sheet of paper – collect any observations without comments – they are not trying to guess what the right scenario is because there isn't one. It is not possible therefore for them to get anything right, not necessary for the facilitator to give credit for any contributions. What you are collecting is a list of observations and possibilities. The idea is to allow – to give the message that it is fine to come up with ideas here.

A useful way to collect what they say is to differentiate between 'what we know' and 'what we are guessing' and make two separate lists on the sheet. For example we know that the woman is sitting down, that she took a bite out of an apple. We are guessing that she is homeless (might be an actor in a film), feeling anxious etc.

Having collected information it is often the case that students are motivated to help in this kind of dramatic scenario.

Ask: 'If we were to approach her and ask her a question – what would we ask?' Then the students come up with questions to ask that will elicit who she is, whether she needs help etc.

They can take it in turns to approach the woman in her shelter and ask her the questions they have decided on.

This can lead to offering help – which will depend upon her answers but might include finding some food for her, or helping to make a better shelter, or seeking help from Social Services, or tracing a friend or family member.

Speaking – P Level 8 – Pupils use conjunctions that suggest cause

PHSE
1. Examine appropriate ways of approaching someone we don't know – what kind of greeting to use, whether to sit down next to her, opposite her, or to remain standing etc.
2. Examine appropriate ways of offering help – without being patronising or interfering.

PHSE – P level 6 – Pupils may show concern for others

PHSE – P Level 7 – Pupils show consideration of the needs and feelings of other people

Storytelling • the woman tells the story of her life as the students sit around her;
              • the students make up a story of what her life might have been to this point and might be in the future.

Literacy –   1. Create a story together of what the woman's situation is. Write the story
collective   of her life to this point.
writing   2. Devise a scenario of what happens to her from this moment in time.

Home on the Street in action

One example of how this environment has been used

I have often used a pared down version of Home on the Street when working with a group for the first time. I find that it provides an opportunity to make a very open invitation to students to contribute possibilities, to make suggestions, without fear of judgement.

In this example I gathered the group round me on the floor sitting on carpet squares. I told them that their teacher would in a minute pretend to be someone else and that she would stand up, put this blanket (I held up the blanket) round her shoulders, pick up this bag (I held it up) and walk into this space and do something. I then asked if they were ready to begin, which they were,★ and invited them to watch and listen and to notice anything that happened. Their teacher then stood up, picked up the blanket, put it round her shoulders in front of them, picked up the bag and prepared to walk into the space.

The setting and props we used were just the blanket and bag. The bag had in it an apple, a bit of paper with a picture of a house and two people crudely drawn on it, a pencil, a brooch and a few foreign coins.

The space into which she walked was a cleared part of the classroom with an un-cluttered wall against which she leaned when she sat down.

The brief for the teacher was: walk into the space, look over your shoulder two or three times to see if anyone is following, find a place to sit, look into your bag, have a look at the picture, take a bite out of the apple, settle down and gradually nod off to sleep. Less than two minutes of action.

When she had done that I stopped the action and asked her to take her blanket off and come and join us. I then said to the group: 'What did we notice? What do we think was happening there?' I put a big piece of paper on the floor in front of me and picked up a pen. Students made suggestions and I wrote them down. Their observations focussed on how she seemed rather than the contents of the bag. We then decided that we would like more information so devised some questions to ask her and got the teacher back into the role of the woman. One by one the students went up and asked her questions that revealed that she was hungry and thirsty. The students offered to go and find food and drink.

★ Had they not been ready I would have taken longer talking about what was going to happen and maybe rehearsed their teacher coming in until they were ready to accept the idea. It is important not to start an activity like this before the students have indicated that they are ready to accept the fiction, the make believe. Any time we take preparing the group for what is to come will be time well spent.

We brought the teacher out of role while the students drew representations of the food and drink on paper. With the teacher back in position the students took the food and drink up to her. We could just as easily have mimed the food and drink but chose to draw them to give another activity and to give concrete examples to the students. Sometimes it is easier for students to believe what is happening when they have made a representation of what they are doing.

The woman thanked them and the session came to an end there.

Suggested learning outcomes

Speaking – P Level 8 – Pupils use conjunctions that suggest cause

PHSE – P Level 6 – Pupils may show concern for others

PHSE – P Level 7 – Pupils show consideration of the needs and feelings of other people

Part 4

Other . . .

Chapter 16

Umbrella Canopy and Umbrella Tent

This chapter is really two environments – Umbrella Canopy and Umbrella Tent. The Canopy is a group activity, the Tent an individual one. They can be used separately or together. The Umbrella Canopy is most suitable to be set up before the students enter. The students can then add to the umbrellas. The Umbrella Tent is ideal for involving students in the making process.

Umbrella Canopy – What is set up as your students enter the room

At the start   In the centre of the room a variety of umbrellas are suspended at different heights from the ceiling. They are of different colours, sizes and textures. Some hang upright others are inverted; some have the original material removed and replaced with coloured and textured fabrics, others have been fashioned to resemble leaves. Lights are focussed on the umbrellas, which are spaced apart to allow students to move between them. Some have small objects hanging from them. Baskets with props and objects are placed on the floor.

Music plays.

Different sensory channels

Visual
- many different colours and shapes of umbrellas;
- the room is quite dark with lights focussed on the umbrellas and baskets;
- shapes of baskets and objects within them;
- movement as the umbrellas gently spin on their strings.

Auditory
- recorded or live music/singing;
- percussive instruments and objects;
- sound of umbrellas being opened and closed.

Kinaesthetic
- students feel objects of different textures and shapes hanging from the umbrellas and in the baskets;
- movement as the umbrellas gently turn on their ropes with objects hanging from their struts.

Olfactory/ gustatory	• scented wooden balls, herbs and aromatic flowers.

Equipment needed

The basic environment
- umbrellas, some for the Canopy plus one for each student if you are using the Tents – different colours and shapes;
- means of suspending umbrellas from above – this could be a camouflage net or ropes across the ceiling;
- string to suspend umbrellas from the net or ropes across the ceiling;
- a selection of baskets (or containers) for collections of objects and materials for making – what these are depends on your purpose.

Visual
- different coloured fabrics and materials to cover the umbrellas;
- lights – stage lights ideal but any domestic directional light will suffice or indeed the lights in the classroom ceiling;
- objects to suit whatever theme you decide to use – a variety of colour, size and shape.

Auditory
- CD player;
- CDs of pre-recorded music;
- percussive instruments, e.g. small bells, shakers etc. to hang from umbrellas to invite sound exploration;
- percussive objects, e.g. kitchen utensils that can be hit or rattled.

Kinaesthetic
- different textures of fabrics;
- a range of textures among the objects in the baskets.

Olfactory/ gustatory
- scented wooden balls;
- herbs;
- flowers.

How to put the Canopy together

1. Collect the materials you need from the above list – you may not need all of them – it will depend on what your purpose is.
2. Tie the camouflage net, ropes or whatever is to be used to suspend the umbrellas from the ceiling. If the umbrellas are quite large it may be best to use ropes that can be tightened by use of the cleat as described in Structures 1, page 11.
3. Make any alterations you wish to the fabric of the umbrellas – maybe replacing original fabric with different colours or textures, adding leaves to simulate woodland etc.
4. Attach a loop to the points of the umbrellas which are to be hung the right way up so that they can be suspended in upright positions.
5. Suspend the umbrellas at different heights above the floor – some upright and others inverted.
6. Hang any objects appropriate to your topic from the struts of the umbrellas – what you include here will, of course, depend on your intention.
7. Attach lengths of fabric and other materials with different colours and textures to the umbrellas.

8. Hang small bells and other percussive objects from the umbrellas.
9. Place scented wooden balls in one or more of the umbrellas.
10. Collect individual students' favourite objects to personalise umbrellas as tents.
11. Place objects in the baskets.

Ways to make use of Umbrella Canopy and Umbrella Tent

Explore the Umbrella Canopy

1. Students walk or wheel their chairs between the umbrellas – observing, touching, using percussive instruments and objects.
2. Exploration can be done all together or one at a time as others watch and listen – when done individually it heightens the experience and makes it more significant as everyone has to wait for their own special moment of exploration.
3. This environment is suitable to be used with students who have PMLD in order to provide them with multi-sensory stimuli.

P Level 1(i)–P3(ii) depending on how interactive and pro-active the pupil is

The Umbrella Tent

1. Each student decorates his/her own umbrella with personal objects that engage him.
2. Each student makes or helps to make decorations for his umbrella.

The umbrella as tent

Figure 23 The Umbrella Tent – for individuals. A student can lie beneath the umbrella and interact with objects hanging from it. The fan adds another sensory experience.

3. Staff assist students as necessary to hang materials and objects that have interested a particular student onto an umbrella.

4. Students make their own umbrella tent by attaching objects they choose from the baskets. Non-ambulant students can lie down on cushions or mats on the floor and see the umbrellas above their heads. Wheelchair users can have their umbrella tied onto the back of their chair and open above their head

Storytelling   The Umbrella Canopy – or a single Umbrella Tent – can be used as a setting for listening to a story. In that case hanging from the umbrella would be objects that relate to the story.

Listening – P level 7 – Pupils listen, attend to and follow stories for short stretches of time

Numeracy   • counting umbrellas to see if there are enough for one each;
            • each umbrella has a number on it and during the exploration of the environment students are invited to follow the number sequence from 1 to 8 or however many umbrellas there are.

Maths Number – P Level 4 – Pupils show awareness of number activities and counting

Art and craft   The students can help in decorating the umbrellas, making animal shapes or plaiting ribbons or choosing fabrics to hang from an umbrella.

Umbrella Tent in action

One example of how this environment has been used

We used the Umbrella Tent at the end of a two-day multi-sensory exploration as a way of concluding the activities. The students all had profound and multiple learning difficulties and had been working and playing with their parents and carers using a variety of multi-sensory activities.

At the end of the two days each family was given a large golf-style brightly coloured umbrella (which we had found in a pound shop for, you guessed it, £1 each!) and the parents decorated it with all the objects that their child had particularly liked and engaged with during the sessions.

The child then lay down on a mat with their head under the umbrella that was resting on the floor (see Figure 23 above). Then as they engaged again with the objects a violin played soothing music to bring the project to an end in a relaxed way.

I know that one of the families was still using their umbrella some years later. When they go on holiday the umbrella folds up and goes with them so that their daughter has her own mobile multi-sensory environment whenever she wants it.

Suggested learning outcomes

P Level 1(i)–P3(ii) depending on how interactive and pro-active the pupil is

Maths Number – P Level 4 – Pupils show awareness of number activities and counting

Listening – P level 7 – Pupils listen, attend to and follow stories for short stretches of time

Chapter 17

Rotary Washing Line

Rotary Washing Line can be set up before the students enter or you can involve them in the decision making during the set up. Which you choose will depend on your purpose.

What is set up as your students enter the room

At the start   At the centre of the room is a rotary clothes line. Different coloured items of washing, including sheets and a variety of clothing, hang down from the arms of the rotary clothes line.

On the floor beneath and around the line are mats, duvets, cushions and other comfortable surfaces. They are arranged round the base of the pole like spokes of a wheel with the pole as centre.

The atmosphere is relaxing. The room is softly lit with some lights focussed on the brightly coloured sheets and clothes.

A fan wafts the clothes on the line.

Soft flute music is playing in the background.

The smell of soap and washing powder hangs in the air.

Students enter and lie on the floor beneath the clothes line.

Different sensory channels

Visual
- clothes, fabrics and ribbons of different colours, shape, size and texture hang from the rotary clothes line, rotating slowly;
- the room is softly lit with lights focussed onto the clothes hanging from the line;
- mats, duvets and cushions laid out around the pole to provide soft surfaces for students and staff to lie down on.

Auditory
- soft flute music is played live or from a CD player.

Kinaesthetic
- different mats, duvets, cushions laid out around the pole have different textures that students can feel;
- washing hangs so that it is within reach of students;
- some ribbons and other different materials hang down to a level where the students can touch them;
- breeze from a fan.

Olfactory/ gustatory	•	scented soap and detergent kept near a fan provides the smell of freshly washed clothes.

Equipment needed

The basic environment	• a rotary clothes line; • a means to support the rotary line – the concrete base from a garden parasol or a netball post or equivalent.
Visual	• sheets – different colours; • clothing of different shapes and sizes from children's socks to boiler suits and everything in between; • ribbons and other textured materials to hang; • lights preferably with focus but any light source will enhance the atmosphere; • domestic anglepoise light; • torches.
Auditory	• flute (or other soothing) music live or recorded; • a CD player; • fan or wind machine.
Kinaesthetic	• mats and cushions of different shapes, size and texture for students to feel and use; • pillows and duvets.
Olfactory/ gustatory	• soap; • scented detergent; • perfumes.

How to put it together

1. Collect the materials you need from the above list – you may not need all of them – it will depend on what your purpose is.
2. Anchor the rotary washing line in the concrete base (or whatever you are using).
3. Place the line into the base and secure it so that it will rotate.
4. Hang the clothes and different coloured sheets/materials on the lines.
5. Add any strips of ribbon and other fabrics. If you want students to focus mainly on the visual experience of lights through fabric then the clothes etc. need to be short. If however you are going to include a kinaesthetic experience then they need to nearly touch the floor so that students can reach them.
6. Lay mats, duvets, cushions and other comfortable surfaces under and around the line for students to lie on.
7. Lighting – place a direct light through the material from above. This is most easily done where there are stage lights in the roof; however different effects can be made by shining a domestic anglepoise lamp through the washing from above.
8. Position the fan or wind machine to blow the clothes.
9. Have torches to hand for other visual effects.
10. Set up the CD player.

Ways to make use of the Rotary Washing Line

Art and
design
activities

Students can be involved in making this environment:

• simple activities like selecting the cloths and ribbons to hang from the lines;
• more complex activities, like plaiting different coloured ribbons or strips of cloth together to hang from the lines;
• positioning of the mats, duvets and cushions;
• positioning of lights to shine through the coloured fabrics on the lines.

P Level 3(i) – Pupils begin to communicate intentionally

P Level 3(ii) – Pupils may respond to options and choices with actions or gesture

P Level 6 – Pupils show an intention to create

Explore and
experience
the
environment

For relaxing. The students lie on the mats and suitable supportive cushions with their heads towards the centre of the pole like the spokes of a wheel.

Gentle music is played – either live or recorded. Quiet and slow music will create a calming atmosphere.

The rotary line is then turned slowly to give a soothing and calming experience.

To energise. To raise the energy and have lots of fun and laughter the rotary line can have lots of long ribbons etc. hanging from it and be spun round at high speed with fast music playing. The students can be in wheelchairs and chairs or on the mats on the floor.

P Level 1(i)–P3(ii) depending on how interactive and pro-active the pupil is

---

Storytelling

This environment could be used in a similar way to Chapter 2, Sari Tent (page 35) for storytelling. For this purpose it might be more suitable for students to sit in a circle round the pole.

To meet a
character

It could also be used in a similar way to Chapter 6, the Laundry (page 59) to meet:

The laundry woman who works here appears (from behind the washing lines). She invites the students to help her because she has so much to do. She asks them if they will help her:

• sort the clothes;
• pair up the socks;
• take the pegs off the line;
• gather clothes together when the wind gets up and a storm threatens;
• hold the clothes out to dry in the wind from the fan.

Rotary Washing Line in action

One example of how this environment has been used

This was used on a residency with students who have profound and multiple learning difficulties and their parents. The theme of the residency was 'washing' so the rotary line had earlier been used to peg washing on to dry.

We used it in this way to create a calming experience for the group at the end of the day. We covered the washing lines with coloured fabric and shone lights through it from above. Parents and children lay down under it on cushions (as described above). We brought the lights down low and a musician played gentle music on her flute. The line was turned slowly first in one direction and then the other, so that the different coloured materials moved above the people underneath.

This exercise lasted for about 15 minutes, after which people were wonderfully relaxed and some were asleep!

Suggested learning outcomes

P Level 1(i)–P3(ii) depending on how interactive and pro-active the pupil is

Art – P Level 3(i) – Pupils begin to communicate intentionally

P Level 3(ii) – Pupils may respond to options and choices with actions or gesture

Art – P Level 6 – Pupils show an intention to create

Chapter 18

Garden Pond

The students can be involved in creating the setting for the garden pond; however it is an activity particularly suited to the PMLD end of the spectrum so it might be best to set it up before the students arrive.

What is set up as your students enter the room

At the start   In the centre of the room a garden pond with rocks around its edge. In the centre of the pond a small fountain sends a vertical spray half a metre into the air. The surface of the water shimmers and reflects light.

Around the pond pot plants and flowers and a string of fairy lights create an exotic garden setting.

The sound of water from the fountain can be heard.

The students gather in a circle round the pond.

Different sensory channels

Visual
- water pond with fountain;
- light reflects off the water surface;
- fairy lights;
- different shades of green from the plants (real or imitation) and colours from flowers.

Auditory
- the sounds of water and fountain;
- splashing sound caused by hands and feet in the water;
- a whole variety of sounds when the water is moved, sprayed or rippled.

Kinaesthetic
- dangling hands or feet into the water;
- varying temperatures can be introduced.

Olfactory/ gustatory
- the air carries a smell of perfume;
- scent of flowers;
- drinking and tasting water (not from the pond!) can be part of the experience.

Equipment needed

The basic environment	• a watertight container is needed – a children's paddling pool, a tin bath or a bucket depending on the purpose; • water; • buckets or hosepipe to bring the water to the pond; • garden fountain and 13 amp socket.
Visual	• rocks or plastic bin liners stuffed with paper to look like rocks; • other stones or pebbles; • plants; • flowers; • fairy lights.
Auditory	• a small garden pump to create the fountain; • most of the auditory experience of this environment will be made by student activity in the pond – with hands or feet.
Kinaesthetic	• collections of glass pebbles; • strings for threading beads onto; • beads – selection of colours and sizes.
Olfactory/ gustatory	• rose petals; • perfume; • additional water to drink.

How to put it together

1. Collect the materials you need from the above list – you may not need all of them – it will depend on what your purpose is.
2. Cover the area round and under the pond with a plastic sheet.
3. Put the empty container you are using in position (it will be more difficult to move a pond of any size when the water is in it).
4. If you want to create something that is part of a theme you may wish to disguise the container. For example a plastic paddling pool can be disguised by laying green or brown material over its sides to simulate garden or beach. To create a rock pool you can stuff plastic bin liners with paper to represent rocks and lay them over the edge of the paddling pool.
5. The pool is then ready to be filled with water either by a hosepipe or carrying buckets. For a more Mediterranean rock pool, or if some of your students are sensitive to cold, you can add some warm water.
6. Place the plants and flowers and anything else you are using round the pond.
7. For an added sensory experience you can introduce a small pump like the ones used in garden ponds. The water will need to be a certain depth for the pump to work. This gives moving water and a fountain that students often love to put their hands into as well as the calming sound of running water.

Ways to make use of the Garden Pond

Art activities 1. The students can help in preparing and setting up the rocks, plants and flowers around the pond.

2. Threading beads onto strings and hanging them from plants that over-hang the water so that the lengths of beads dangle into the water.

Explore the • the students can dip their hands in, go for a paddle;

garden pond • watch the water from the fountain playing on the surface of the pond;

• float objects on the pond – paper boats, lilies, rose petals;

• drop coloured glass pebbles into the water.

P Level 2(ii) – Pupils co-operate with shared exploration and supported participation

Storytelling Students can sit around the pond and listen to stories. If there was a voyage across the sea or a river crossing in the story this could be enacted by passing a model boat across the water.

Reading – P Level 4 – Pupils listen and respond to familiar rhymes and stories

Numeracy 1. Volume experiments – how much do different containers hold in relation to each other?

2. Pouring water from one container to another.

Maths Using and Applying – P Level 4 – Pupils show awareness of changes in quantity

Other This environment can be used in conjunction with Chapter 21, Herb
activities Garden (page 137).

Garden Pond in action

One example of how this environment has been used

Garden Pond, with a few modifications, can also be used as a farmyard pond or, as in this example, a rock pool on the beach.

This example is taken from a Bamboozle residency for children with profound and complex needs and their parents and was intended for use as a relaxed multi-sensory exploration. We used a child's paddling pool and draped the sides with green bin liners to represent seaweed-covered rocks. We introduced sand, pebbles and shells into the bottom of the pool and spread some more sand around the outer edges of the pool to represent the beach on which we put deck chairs, sun cream, buckets, spades and other items people take to the beach.

Parents and children then took turns to experience the pool in any way they liked. Some brought wheelchairs up to the side of the pool and put the sand and shells on the child's tray, filled buckets full of water and allowed their child to put hands and feet into it. We varied the temperature of the water by pouring in buckets of hot water into the rock pool. Others got their child out of the chair and put their feet directly into the pool, poured sand over their hands and feet, listened to conch shells, rubbed sun cream onto arms and legs etc.

Suggested learning outcomes

P Level 2(ii) – Pupils co-operate with shared exploration and supported participation

Reading – P Level 4 – Pupils listen and respond to familiar rhymes and stories

Maths Using and Applying – P Level 4 – Pupils show awareness of changes in quantity

Chapter 19

Bomb Site – World War II

This environment is very suitable for involving the students in helping to set it up. Whether you do involve them or bring them into the bomb site already set up will depend on your intention.

What is set up as your students enter the room

At the start   While the students are waiting outside the room there is the sound of an air raid siren. The sound fades away. Silence.

The 'all-clear' siren sounds. The students enter one by one. They are invited to find a place to sit down among mounds – on chairs or carpet squares. They are asked not to touch anything yet.

Inside the room, around the three walls opposite the door is a semi-circle of corrugated card that provides a neutral backdrop. Within the space created by the card are several mounds of varying shapes and sizes. There is space to move between the mounds that are covered by dust sheets. It is not clear what is under the dust sheets.

Different sensory channels

Visual
- shapes of the initial landscape of mounds;
- objects beneath the mounds;
- smoke.

Auditory
- air raid siren;
- all-clear siren.

Kinaesthetic
- handling objects;
- emotional content of 'Drama' and 'Meet a character' activities.

Equipment needed

This is a simple environment to create. The majority of the time involved will be in the assembling of objects to use in the exploration.

The basic Environment	• corrugated card for the semi-circular backdrop – or neutral fabric to hang over the three walls of the room; • dust sheets – decorators' dust sheets have a suitable texture but any plain sheets will do the job; • tables and chairs to make the body of the mounds to be covered – the mounds represent bombed out buildings;
Visual	Everyday objects: the more 'period' they are the more authentic the experience for students. However if the purpose is to empathise with the predicament of people who might have lost their homes then the authenticity or the precise origin of the artefacts is not so important. • World War II artefacts; • children's toys; • kitchen utensils; • household objects; • clothes of the period; • smoke machine.
Auditory	• CD player; • recording of an air raid siren and the all-clear siren.
Kinaesthetic	• this will depend on what you are introducing as objects hidden beneath the mounds.
For drama idea/s or meeting a character	• a basic costume for an Air Raid Precaution (ARP) warden – a helmet or arm band with ARP on it would do the job; • item of costume for a person searching the rubble – perhaps an old fashioned apron for a woman or a trilby hat for a man.

How to put it together

1. Collect the materials you need from the above list.
2. Erect the corrugated card as backdrop – or hang the plain cloths to cover the walls and make the space neutral.
3. Turn some of the classroom tables and chairs over to make the mounds of 'rubble' to cover.
4. Place any objects and artefacts among the rubble (under tables, chairs and any other obstacle being used to create the shapes).
5. Cover the mounds with dust sheets.
6. Put the CD player with air-raid siren and 'all-clear' recordings in place.

Ways to make use of the Bomb Site

Explore environment	• move among the rubble; • search under the rubble for possessions.
Drama	This makes an ideal setting for: • finding out more about the effect of bombing on London or Cologne or anywhere else that has experienced that sort of warfare;

- a PHSE session concerning loss – where a woman (teacher or TA in role) comes to the bombed-out street looking for their house or belongings or a loved one;
- students to devise questions to ask the woman.

English Listening – P Level 8 – Pupils take part in role play with confidence

PHSE – P Level 6 – Pupils may show concern for others

Meet a
character
1. Watch the ARP warden searching the rubble for any survivors and then ask him about what he has to do.
2. Watch the woman searching the rubble – freeze the action (i.e. get the woman to stand still and maintain her expression) then wonder with the students what that expression might mean. What might she be feeling at this moment in time?
3. Question either of these characters about their experiences of the war.

English Speaking – P Level 6 – Pupils initiate and maintain short conversations. They ask simple questions to obtain information

Literacy
- write (or draw or record in other ways) a list of the findings on the bomb site;
- make a list of the emotions that might be experienced by the woman exploring the bombed out street looking for what she has lost.

National Curriculum Writing Level 1

Bomb Site in action

One example of how this environment has been used

When working with practitioners at the Imperial War Museum (IWM) we used this environment as a setting in which visiting school groups could interact with World War II artefacts. As you might imagine the IWM has a lot of such artefacts. The aim of this session was to find a creative way for students to handle and examine the artefacts.

When school groups visit the Churchill Rooms (part of the IWM) for a workshop they work in a classroom that has tables and chairs. We turned these over and piled them up making a variety of shapes that we covered with dust sheets.

We then arranged a number of artefacts in the 'bomb site' setting; some concealed, some partially concealed and some entirely visible.

We then divided the room with drapes in such a way that there was a space for the students to assemble at one end of the classroom so that they could not see the mounds which represented the rubble of a bombed street at the other.

When the students gathered we invited them to consider that they were members of the emergency services arriving in a street that had received a direct hit during the recent bombing raid. We told them that their first job was to find any possessions that they could and bring them to a central collecting point. One of the IWM workshop leaders then appeared in an Air Raid Precaution (ARP) warden's costume and started the drama by sounding the all-clear siren by winding the handle of one of the actual sirens from World War II. The students then entered the space to look for the artefacts.

When they returned with what they had found there was a discussion about how each artefact came to be where it had been found. This gave the students the opportunity to handle and speculate about the uses of the artefacts. Where they were unsure of the uses of some of the items their 'boss' the ARP warden explained the use to them. Getting an expert in role to give the information in this way is a useful way to provide information and expertise.

Suggested learning outcomes

English Speaking – P Level 6 – Pupils initiate and maintain short conversations. They ask simple questions to obtain information

English Listening – P Level 8 – Pupils take part in role play with confidence

PHSE – P Level 6 – Pupils may show concern for others

National Curriculum Writing Level 1

Chapter 20

Woodland Floor

This environment is best set up before the students enter.

What is set up as your students enter the room

At the start   The centre of the room has a circle of bark chips spread about 5 centimetres thick. In the centre of the circle a group of plants.

There are sounds of the forest. Birdsong and the scream of monkeys can be heard.

The smell of damp, fresh bark chip fills the air.

Different sensory channels

Visual   • thick layer of bark chip.

Auditory   • CD plays pre-recorded music of sounds of the forest including birdsong and sounds of monkeys.

Kinaesthetic   • students can handle the bark chip and walk barefoot on it to experience the touch of the chip and the damp feeling on hands and feet.

Olfactory/   • smell of the fresh damp bark chip.
gustatory

Equipment needed

The basic   • plastic sheet on which the bark chip is laid;
environment   • bark chip.

Visual   • plants;
                • objects for hide-and-seek activity.

Auditory   • CD to play pre-recorded woodland sounds.

Kinaesthetic   • bark chip;
                • objects for hide-and-seek.

Olfactory/   • scent of bark chip.
gustatory

How to put it together

1. Collect the materials you need from the above list.
2. Decide whether to cover a small area or the whole space. This will depend on your purpose. If what you are doing is creating a multi-sensory experience then a small area in the corner of the room will suffice; if however it is part of a bigger project then there is the possibility of covering a much larger area.
3. Put down heavy duty black plastic first – this enables you to put this environment in a carpeted classroom as the plastic – as long as it is heavy duty – is unlikely to tear.
4. Empty the bags of bark chip onto the plastic and spread to the depth you want it. When the bark first comes out of the bags it is often damp so spreading it out the day before you want to use it will enable it to dry out a bit.
5. Place the plants in position.
6. Have any objects to hand that you are using for hide-and-seek or other activities.
7. Position the CD player for the sound track.

Ways to make use of the Woodland Floor

Art activities • students move the bark chip around to make patterns on the floor in the manner of finger painting but on a larger scale;
• students sit in a circle round the bark chip. Each student in turn crosses the circle making a trail across the floor.

Art – P Level 4 – Pupils show awareness of cause and effect in a creative process. They make marks intentionally on a surface

Explore the • students walk barefoot and experience the feel of the forest floor. If it is
Woodland   big enough they can have a place to move around and sit down in a
Floor   circle to hear stories;
• listen to the sounds and breathe in the smell with eyes closed to heighten the sensory experience.

P Level 3(i) – Pupils participate in shared activities with less support. They explore materials in increasingly complex ways

Storytelling   The experience of any story that involves woodland, forest or jungle can be enhanced by the smell and texture of the bark chip. *The Gruffalo, Robin Hood, Hansel and Gretel* etc.

English Reading – P Level 4 – Pupils listen and respond to familiar rhymes and stories

Hide-and-seek   Bury objects in the bark chip for students to find.

Woodland Floor in action

One example of how this environment has been used

The contents of a bag of bark chip scattered on the floor is a simple way to enhance the multi-sensory nature of many environments that you can create. It adds texture and smell very quickly.

Bamboozle has used this idea as part of many environments, including several described in this book. For example with Chapter 1, Musical Forest and Chapter 4, Rainforest Jungle we spread bark chip beneath the hanging trees to give the sound of crunching as the bark is trodden on or wheeled over, and to add the olfactory experience that newly opened bags of bark chip provide.

In Chapter 12, Trenches of World War I (see Figure 21, page 95) and Chapter 23, Border Crossing we used it as a scattering along the bottom of the corrugated card sides of the trench and around the gateway through the border to give additional texture.

For Chapter 22, Circle of Straw Bales, the light scattering of woodchip gave the impression of a farmyard that hens could peck around.

With Chapter 18, Garden Pond and Chapter 21, Herb Garden the bark chip is more integral to the environment and we made use of it *as* bark chip rather than as a way of giving an impression of the forest floor, farmyard or border post.

Suggested learning outcomes

P Level 3(i) – Pupils participate in shared activities with less support. They explore materials in increasingly complex ways

Art – P Level 4 – Pupils show awareness of cause and effect in a creative process. They make marks intentionally on a surface

English Reading – P Level 4 – Pupils listen and respond to familiar rhymes and stories

Chapter 21

Herb Garden

The students can be involved in making the herb garden by piling the earth and planting the herbs, or the garden can be set up for them to come into.

What is set up as your students enter the room

At the start In the centre of the room a circle of earth is piled up with a border of woodchip round the edge of it. Outside the circle are carpet squares, mats or cushions for the students to sit on.

Around the circle between the mats are herbs in small pots. Their scent fills the air.

Soft music plays.

Different sensory channels

Visual	• earth pit made by piling earth 15–20 cms deep on a black round plastic sheet; • different shapes, colours and sizes of the herb plants; • puppets of bird, snake, ladybird or any other; • any objects to bury under the bark chip or soil.
Auditory	• soft music – live if available – flute or violin would work well.
Kinaesthetic	• handling earth and bark chip; • herbs provide a variety of textures to touch and feel – from scratchy rosemary to soft sage; • handling puppets; • handling objects which are to be hidden.
Olfactory/ gustatory	• smell of the earth and bark chip; • smell and taste of the herbs.

Equipment needed

The basic
environment
• large circular sheet of thick plastic to spread out under the earth pit;
• earth or potting compost – enough to pile 15–20 cms high;
• bark chip.

Visual	• puppets – bird, snake, ladybird or any other; • objects to hide – whatever objects are suitable for your learning outcomes.
Auditory	• violin or flute music – or any soft music; • CD player if recorded music being used.
Kinaesthetic	• garden tools – trowel and forks for students to plant herbs.
Olfactory/ gustatory	• herbs growing in small pots.
For meeting a character or puppet	• some items of costume to represent the gardener – gardening gloves, a rake, a hat or apron; • a stool that the gardener can sit on to be close to the level of the students; • puppets that might be found in a garden, e.g. snake, bird, ladybird.

How to put it together

1. Collect the materials you need from the above list.
2. Put a circular sheet of thick plastic down to protect the carpet or floor from the earth.
3. Then pile the earth or potting compost in the centre and spread it out to about 15–20 cms in depth. This allows enough depth of soil to accommodate small plants that can be kept in the pots and concealed in the soil or taken out and planted in the earth. Which you choose depends on how long the earth pit is going to be there, and what activities you are going to involve the students in. If you want the students to come into a magical garden as part of a story for example, then you may want to plant them beforehand.
4. Then add a circle of bark chip round the edge of the earth. This gives a different texture and can be touched and handled before experiencing the earth itself. Bark chip is also good for hiding objects in to be found later because it does not stick to the objects as soil can.
5. If you are concerned about the earth and bark chip spreading beyond the designated circle then form an edge by rolling up the rim of the black plastic to create a small barrier.

Ways to make use of the Herb Garden

Students help to set up the environment	Students can help get the soil and woodchip out of the bags and pile it up, and decide on positions of the herb plants.
Explore the herb garden	• students can spend time experiencing the feel of the woodchip and soil; • herbs can be passed round to touch and smell and possibly taste; • students can plant the herbs or if more appropriate give directions (verbally or by pointing or eye accessing) to the gardener about where they are to go.

P Level 1(ii) – Pupils show emerging awareness of activities and experiences. They have periods when they appear alert and ready to focus their attention on objects or parts of objects

Puppetry   Each student is visited by a puppet that emerges from under the woodchip where it has been buried – e.g. a snake or a ladybird.

As a setting   Students could meet the gardener who gets them to help plant the herbs
to meet a   and explains to them how to do it.
character

Listening – P Level 4 – Pupils respond appropriately to simple requests which contain one key word

Cooking   Selected herbs are picked and used in cooking activities in the school – these could be taken to the school kitchen or used for classroom cooking activities.

Herb Garden in action

One example of how this environment has been used

We use this in a variety of forms when working with children who have profound and complex needs and their parents and carers. The idea in this example was to give students plenty of time to interact with different items in the garden and have a rich and relaxed multi-sensory experience.

Many of the students in this particular group were wheelchair users so time was spent helping them out of their chairs onto mats and beanbags around the circle of bark chip and earth. While this was being done we introduced live violin music. Having the music live enabled the violinist to move round and be close to each student in turn, so that they experienced the vibrations of the instrument as well as the sound. The students spent time experiencing the feel of the woodchip and soil on hands and feet (with shoes and socks off) and smelling the herbs that were planted in the soil in pots so that the pots could be picked up and moved close to the student where necessary.

We then sang an improvised song about the herb garden and earth pit that included each child's name and what they were doing. For example 'We're sitting round the earth pit and Emily is smelling the herbs'.

Each student was visited by three puppets – a snake that had been buried beneath the bark chip and then emerged, and a bird and a ladybird that had been hidden among the herbs.

Figure 24 A bird puppet and student have an intimate conversation during Bamboozle's interactive touring production of 'Crazy Hair', adapted from Neil Gaiman's book of the same name.

Suggested learning outcomes

P Level 1(ii) – Pupils show emerging awareness of activities and experiences. They have periods when they appear alert and ready to focus their attention on objects or parts of objects

Listening – P Level 4 – Pupils respond appropriately to simple requests which contain one key word

Chapter 22

Circle of Straw Bales

This simple environment gives a different feel to sitting in a circle for story, discussion or to watch an activity and is best suited to being set up before the students enter.

What is set up as your students enter the room

At the start   A circle or semi-circle of straw bales with spaces between each one. A scattering of hay across the floor in the circle creates a farmyard feel.

The sounds of the farmyard – a cock crowing, sheep bleating and a horse's whinny.

Different sensory channels

Visual	• the straw bales; • scattered hay; • animal puppets; • animal masks.
Auditory	• sound of straw and hay as people sit or walk on it; • recorded sounds of the farmyard.
Kinaesthetic	• touch of the straw and hay; • eggs to collect in baskets.
Olfactory/ gustatory	• smell of the hay; • smell of straw; • taste and smell of fruit from the orchard.

Equipment needed

How much equipment you need will depend on your purpose. If you are simply using it as a different setting for storytelling then just the bales will be needed. If it is part of a term-long project about, for example, the Victorians then you may wish to include some or all of the other elements.

The basic environment	• straw bales (these are cheaper than hay – usually half the price).
Visual	• baskets for putting fruit in; • plates or paper napkins to distribute fruit to students.
Auditory	• CD player; • CD of farmyard sound effects.
Kinaesthetic	• hay bale – one hay bale divided up makes plenty of hay to roll in! • breath from the nostrils of the horse's head mask; • eggs – wooden or polystyrene egg shapes.
Olfactory/ gustatory	• a small amount of hay will allow the students to smell it – a whole bale is only necessary if you plan to roll around in it; • fruit for tasting; • knives for cutting up fruit; • plates or bowls to put fruit on; • paper napkins or towels for cleaning hands.
For drama idea/s	• basic costume item for farmer. If historical then a smock or hessian sack tied round the waist as an apron has a timeless feel. For present day overalls and a baseball style cap.
Puppetry	• materials for making animal puppets or masks; • a puppet for interacting with ASD students – and others.

How to put it together

1. Collect the materials you need from the above list – you may not need all of them – it will depend on what your purpose is.
2. Place the straw bales in the circle or however you want to use them. A semi-circle is a good layout if the group is going to watch something.
3. Have any props and puppets to hand.

Ways to make use of the Circle of Straw Bales

Explore environment	1. Rolling or lying in a pile of hay is a much-loved activity for most children. 2. Crawling through a tunnel made of straw bales. Put two bales end to end then place two more parallel to them and about one bale's width apart. Then put three or four other bales across the gap to complete the tunnel. (See Figure 7, page 19.) 3. Handle the hay and straw – its texture, the sound it makes, the smell. 4. Hide the eggs behind the bales and among the hay for students to search for – one group of students can hide them for others to find.

English Listening – P Level 4 – Pupils respond appropriately to simple requests which contain one key word

Tell stories   The circle of bales is an ideal layout for storytelling or discussion. Wheelchair users can park between the bales and be in the circle.

Meet a   A teacher in role as a farmer tells the students about the daily life on the
character   farm – this can be a present day farm or be used for a history topic on Victorians for example.

English Speaking – P Level 6 – Pupils initiate and maintain short conversations using their preferred medium of communication. They ask simple questions to obtain information

Making   1. This is a suitable environment to introduce a puppet of a farmyard
puppets   animal – a horse's head mask or a cat puppet.
or masks   2. If using a horse's head then by attaching a tube from the person wearing
                   the mask to the horse's nostrils you can achieve the archetypal horse's
                   breath experience for the student.
                3. Putting mock suede onto the nose of the horse gives a realistic feel of a
                   horse's muzzle.

Interacting   A member of staff operates a puppet for students to interact with. This can
with   be an effective way of enabling some students on the ASD spectrum to
puppets   engage with the environment. One way of achieving this is for the staff
                member to have no desire to get a 'result'. We have found that when we get

Figure 25 Two students attend to the horse in its stable before offering it a carrot.

Figure 26 This boy on the autistic spectrum is captivated by the duck puppet and gives it his full and calm attention. This was unusual for him and the calmness may have come from the puppeteer's lack of need to get him to interact. Until he made the decision to approach the duck the puppeteer and duck were busy looking round the farmyard with no intention other than to find food. They were not trying to reach the boy's world they were content to wait. And if he came to their world then was the time to give him attention.

the puppet to investigate the environment itself with no evident desire to interact with the student it draws the ASD student in (see Figure 26).

P Level 2(i) – Pupils begin to show interest in people, events or objects

Numeracy
- measuring the size of the bales;
- fractions of fruit as the fruit is cut into pieces for tasting.

Art and craft
- making masks of farm animals;
- examining patterns of cut fruit.

Olfactory/ gustatory
Fruit from the farm orchard – apples and pears or any fruit that is in season can be used. Cut up the fruit into small pieces and encourage students to identify by smell before choosing some to taste.

Figure 27
A boy completely suspends his disbelief to feed the horse puppet. The puppeteer can blow down tubes that run from the puppeteer's position in the horse's neck to its mouth so that the boy can feel the hot breath of the horse. She then reaches her arm through the structure of the head to take the carrot as it is fed into the horse's mouth.

Circle of Straw Bales in action

One example of how this environment has been used

Bales are a very effective way of quickly defining a space which we made use of when the National Theatre commissioned Bamboozle to work with London special schools on the NT production of *War Horse*. This project involved week-long residencies in schools after which the students went to see the production at the National. For some students, sitting in the audience was not the best way to access the play so a day on the Olivier stage was arranged for them with some of the cast, puppeteers and technical crew. The Olivier stage is a huge area and we wanted to find a quick and simple way of defining a manageable space for the activities. A circle of straw bales. These were quick to put in place and reflected the farmyard setting in which Michael Morpurgo's story begins; and the students had seen straw bales in schools already so were familiar with them.

The students and staff were able to sit in a circle on the bales with gaps to accommodate wheelchair users and to allow the horse puppets to enter the space and meet the students.

Suggested learning outcomes

P Level 2(i) – Pupils begin to show interest in people, events or objects

English Listening – P Level 4 – Pupils respond appropriately to simple requests which contain one key word

English Speaking – P Level 6 – Pupils initiate and maintain short conversations using their preferred medium of communication. They ask simple questions to obtain information

Chapter 23

Border Crossing

Border Crossing has most impact if set up before the students arrive. However for some students, particularly those with EBD, it can work well to involve the students in the building of it.

What is set up as your students enter the room

At the start   As students wait outside the room the sound of distant small arms fire can be heard.

They enter. A ramshackle fence. Not a formal political border crossing but a guerrilla style blockade built from assorted materials – lengths of timber, oil drums, pieces of discarded fencing held together with rope and wire. Threaded through and over the whole length of the fence is barbed wire. Tied at various points on the fence are what appear to be trophies, including a doll, a teddy bear, a hat, a pair of binoculars.

There is a narrow gap in the fence across which at waist height is a rail, obstructing passage through.

At a makeshift table, with a scarf concealing part of his face, sits a guard with a rifle leaning beside him. When the students are settled in front of the scene the guard gets up – picks up binoculars and scans the horizon. He is looking to see if anyone is approaching.

Different sensory channels

Visual
- the shapes of the component parts of the fence;
- the actions of the guard;
- the contents of the bags and cases.

Auditory
- recordings of distant small arms fire;
- listening to the dialogue and explanations.

Kinaesthetic
- handling the materials that make up the fence;
- emotional engagement with the people who approach the border crossing.

Equipment needed

How much equipment you need will depend on how complex you want to make the environment. If it is being put up for a short time you might decide just to have a couple of posts with barbed wire over them to represent the crossing. If it is going to be in situ for a couple of weeks or a whole term then it may well be worth the time and trouble to build the complete fence with crossing.

The basic environment	• four upright poles/posts (see Structures 3, page 12) give you one for each side of the gap and one at each end – but less will do;
	• planks of wood;
	• wooden poles;
	• rope/string to tie fence together;
	• hammer and nails for assembling timber parts of fence;
	• miscellaneous available materials that might be part of such a ramshackle construction.
Visual	• assorted objects to tie into the fence as trophies of people who have passed this way before;
	• a flag;
	• binoculars.
Auditory	• recording of distant small arms fire.
Kinaesthetic	• imitation barbed wire.
Olfactory/ gustatory	• a sprinkling of bark chip will give a scent as well as creating a sense of 'otherness' – of being somewhere else.
For drama idea/s	• costume item/s for the guard – a guerrilla-style head scarf;
	• rifle;
	• pack of cards;
	• tin mug;
	• a bag or suitcase for the person who approaches the border post;
	• other cases or bags for groups of students to explore;
	• personal possessions to go in the bags/suitcases;
	• trophies to attach to the border post – these can be photos, items of clothing, a teddy bear etc. – anything to relate to a teaching outcome or to heighten the possibilities of the drama.

How to put it together

1. Collect the materials you need from the above list – you may not need all of them – it will depend on what your purpose is.
2. Erect the upright posts to which the component parts of the fence will be attached.
3. Add other collected materials to make the fence.
4. Finally add the barbed wire – although imitation the wire is made of plastic so the points are not entirely benign.
5. Attach some trophies to the fence.
6. Fill suitcases and bags with personal possessions and place within the environment.
7. Set up a CD player for sound effects of gunfire.

Ways to make use of Border Crossing

Students
build the
border
crossing

A suitable activity for students who are sometimes difficult to engage is to get them building. Before the students arrive have the basic structure of the fence in place. Some upright posts to attach things to for example. Assemble the materials that are to be used to complete the task.

When the students arrive give them the brief – 'We need a rough and ready fence that looks as if it is designed to stop people getting past – and it needs a gap or gate in the middle which will allow passage through.' Then allow them to make decisions about what goes where. We find that the more leeway you allow students (within certain parameters) the more engaged they become with the activity, and the more likely they are to buy into the drama or story.

Design and Technology – P Level 4 – With help pupils begin to assemble components provided for an activity

Design and Technology – P Level 8 – Pupils begin to contribute to decisions about what they will do and how

Explore
environment

Time can be taken to investigate how the border post is constructed – to make alterations, add elements to it, take things away.

Drama

Teacher or TA takes on the role of the guard at the border crossing. The guard is lounging, maybe sitting playing cards, making tea, any ordinary activity. After a few moments the guard picks up binoculars and scans the road leading to the border post. He/she is looking to see if anyone is approaching.

Devising
questions

Students observe the guard for a while. Then you pause the action and the guard comes out of role. Students get into small groups, discuss what they have seen and make up questions to ask the guard to find out about what the job of guarding the gap in the fence entails. You can make up any scenario for the guard to divulge that will serve your purposes – your learning outcomes. It works well to keep it simple and non-specific as it leaves more room for the students' imagination. For example: the guard is simply doing what he has been told – doesn't know the details. It's often boring but it's a job etc. etc.

Making up
stories

For this activity you need several bags or suitcases with personal possessions in them. These are placed within the border crossing setting – probably behind the fence.

You explain to the group that these bags have been taken from people who have passed this way before. If you wish to visually demonstrate how this happened then see 'Heighten the drama' below.

Divide the group up into small groups (I'd suggest two to five in each) and give each group a bag and the task of:

1. Examining its contents.
2. Making up a scenario which explains how the person (or people) carrying the bag came to be at this border crossing.
3. Finding a way of explaining to the rest of the group their findings, which could be enacted, drawn or told as a story.

   You can then put the guard back in his original place at the crossing and get each group to enact their scenario.

English Listening – P Level 7 – Pupils attend to and respond to questions from adults and peers about experiences, events and stories

Differen-
tiation

This provides a good opportunity for differentiation. The guard can interrogate more able students quite rigorously. For some students making the approach to the border post might be a significant achievement in itself so they can be allowed to get off lightly!

Heighten
the drama

A person (a second TA) approaches the crossing with a travelling bag and asks to pass through. Without saying anything the guard (holding rifle) relieves the traveller of the bag and empties it on the floor – picks up anything of interest and hangs it with other trophies on the fence – makes the person replace possessions in bag. Takes bag from them and puts it in the pile behind the fence. The guard then shoves the traveller through the gap in the fence and out of sight. It is ambiguous whether the traveller is captured or has been sent on her way without her bag.

English Listening – P Level 8 – Pupils respond appropriately to questions about why or how

Transition
activities

The border post and the challenge for people to get past it can be a metaphor for any of the transitions that students face – from one age group to another, from school to school or from school to life beyond.

Storytelling

This environment would make a suitable backdrop for telling stories of difficult journeys which have challenges along the way.

Literacy

1. Writing the scenarios of the groups exploring what the contents of the bags suggest.
2. Writing dialogue for conversations between guard and traveller.
3. Writing the story of what happened in the dramatic scenes between their traveller and the guard.

National Curriculum Writing Level 1–3

Border Crossing in action

One example of how this environment has been used

Border Crossing was used in this example as a vehicle for incorporating students' individual targets. The situation was that three classes in a school came together for a week's residency to explore the theme of transition. The teachers wanted to see how a drama of this kind could incorporate the existing targets that they had for their pupils. These targets included:

- recognising the numerals 1, 2 and 3 and putting them in order;
- asking for help when needed;
- taking a message accurately from one person to another.

The action in the narrative included a woman (actor in role) recruiting the help of the students to follow her on a dangerous journey. This journey led her to arrive at the border crossing where she had her possessions taken by the guards before being roughly shoved on her way through the border crossing and out of sight. As the students had previously agreed to help the woman they had to find a way to get past the guards. At the beginning of the next day they arrived at the crossing with the intention of persuading the guards to let them through. When the first student arrived at the crossing to try his luck the guard asked him his name. 'James', he answered. The guard went to the fence and found an envelope pegged to it with 'James' on it. 'This must be for you', he said and gave James his envelope. 'Do what it says in there and I might let you pass.' In the envelope were 10 pieces of paper each numbered 1–10, and the instruction, 'Find the first three numbers and put them in order.' The student then had to find help to read the note and follow the instruction. He did this and returned to the guard and demonstrated his ability to put them in order. The guard then let him through. In this way the whole group was able to attempt their target. If right, they went through; if wrong, they were sent back to get help and come and try again.

This provided a way of enabling any target at all to be included in the dramatic narrative and the teachers the chance to evaluate how close their students were to meeting the targets.

Suggested learning outcomes

Design and Technology – P Level 4 – With help pupils begin to assemble components provided for an activity

Design and Technology – P Level 8 – Pupils begin to contribute to decisions about what they will do and how

English Listening – P Level 7 – Pupils attend to and respond to questions from adults and peers about experiences, events and stories

English Listening – P Level 8 – Pupils respond appropriately to questions about why or how

National Curriculum Writing Level 1–3

Section three

Appendices

3.1 Sources of materials

In these days of the Internet, finding pretty much anything you want doesn't take long. The following might be of help to shorten your search for some items and give you ideas for others.

Barbed wire – fake! – available from www.sillyjokes.co.uk
Bark chip, soil and other garden materials – local garden centres or DIY shops.
Camouflage nets – www.surplusandadventure.com
Cardboard boxes – find someone who has recently moved house (packing boxes are sturdy). Appliance stores throw away lots of very large boxes that fridge freezers are delivered in.
Cardboard tubes – most carpet stores will give these away. Good to ring before going to see whether they have just cleared them out.
Carpet squares – most carpet shops are happy to give these away when they have finished with sample books.
Charity shops – worth a look for props and costumes.
Copper pipes – plumbers often throw away off-cuts of copper heating pipes.
Corrugated card – a lot of places sell this online. It is certainly worth shopping around as prices vary immensely.
Costumes – see Props and costumes below.
Newsprint – newspaper printing houses. They throw away dozens of the ends of print rolls each day so are usually willing to give them away. A phone call to your local paper to see where the paper is printed followed by a journey to pick them up will give you a great resource.
Plastic sheets – you can get heavy duty plastic sheeting (usually black) from a builder's yard. It is much better quality and more economical in the long run than buying it from local hardware or DIY stores. You usually have to buy a larger quantity but it lasts a long time.
Props and costumes – if you need authentic looking props or realistic costumes it is worth contacting your local theatre (professional or amateur) which may lend or hire props and costumes.
Pound shops are a great source of materials. We have found, among other things, umbrellas, fibre optic lights, torches, and have sometimes visited a pound shop to see what they've got then built activities around our purchases!

3.2 The author

Christopher Davies is a director, writer and educator and a keen student of linguistics and non-verbal language. He is continually seeking ways in which we can improve our methods of communication with young people for whom making themselves understood is a daily and life-long challenge. His work is informed by three fundamental beliefs:

- that it is his job as an artist and educator to provide all young people with the means to find their own voice;
- that young people of all abilities and disabilities flourish when we remove the judgement from the educative process and enable them to find their own agenda in an environment free from fear;
- that all young people know more than we think they do, are capable of more than they think they are and have the capacity to surprise us all.

This book is an expression of these beliefs in the form of multi-sensory environments and activities that are essential ingredients of an inspirational, balanced and creative curriculum.

Christopher taught in primary schools for 13 years before spending an inspiring year at The Central School of Speech and Drama in London. He then joined the Leicestershire Drama Advisory Service where he ran courses for teachers, worked in special schools and set up youth theatres for students with learning difficulties. He has tutored on Leicester University's MA drama course, run INSET courses nationally and led training workshops for many organisations including The National Theatre, Shakespeare's Globe and the Imperial War Museum. As a director he has created work for the London and Edinburgh Fringe and toured internationally. In 1994 he set up Bamboozle Theatre Company with Sue Pyecroft.

As co-artistic director Christopher facilitates Bamboozle's residencies for schools and families, writes and directs the company's touring shows and runs the acclaimed training programme. He produces resources for use in schools including the book *Dramatic Starts – 17 ways to start a drama session with SEN students.*

Figure 28 Here the author and a student warily approach the horse with an apple.

Index